Abracadabra!

Abracadabra!

How to sell anything to anyone, anytime, anywhere

Mike Lipkin

ZEBRA

ZEBRA

Published by Zebra Press
a division of Struik Publishers (Pty) Ltd
(a member of the Struik Publishing Group (Pty) Ltd)
32 Thora Crescent, Wynberg, Sandton

Reg. No.: 54/00965/07

First published in September 1997

Editor Marika Truter
DTP and cover design Neels Bezuidenhout
Cover photograph Brent Stirton

Reproduction by Disc Express cc, Johannesburg
Printed and bound by CTP Printers (Pty) Ltd, PO Box 6060, Parow East 7501

ISBN 1 86872 081 0

'Magic: an extraordinary or irresistible charm, influence or power; mysteriously enchanting'

— WEBSTER'S UNABRIDGED DICTIONARY OF THE ENGLISH LANGUAGE

'As you let your own light shine, you unconsciously give other people permission to do the same. The future belongs to those who believe in the beauty of their dreams.'

— NELSON MANDELA

Contents

Welcome to the journey – I know you'll enjoy the ride!

Yes!!! I am delighted that you have decided to invest in this book. In fact, I'm more than delighted: I'm ecstatic! I'm juiced! I'm pumped! In return for your trust and money, I promise you that the selling secrets that lie within these pages will massively increase your power to persuade, influence and lead others.

This is my fourth book, but it is the one that I am most excited about. Come to think of it, I'm excited about everything, but especially this book. Somehow the process of growing and building never gets easier. But we do get better at it. I believe that my previous books were merely a foundation for this one. I have installed all my knowledge, experience, insight, pleasure and pain in this book. It's about as close as I will ever come to giving birth.

Do you know what? Every one of us is a salesperson in one way or another. Every single day we share our ideas and beliefs with others. We are constantly talking, listening, relating and giving to and taking from others. But most of us do not see ourselves as 'salespeople'. The very word 'salesperson' seems to create a negative image in many people's minds. This groundbreaking book will change your beliefs on that score.

One of the greatest myths of all time is that knowledge is power. Knowledge is not power. At worst it is a curse. At best it is potential power. Knowledge without the means to share that knowledge effectively with others leads only to frustration, disharmony and even alienation from other people. How many times have you been party to a conversation where the message you thought you sent was not the message received by the other person? How many times have you witnessed people becoming frustrated by their inability to understand what the other person is really trying to say? How many times have you watched two people fail to connect with each other because they were on different wavelengths?

To sell means to persuade, influence and connect deeply with others. There is no power on earth that has a greater impact on the quality of your life than your ability to sell your ideas, knowledge and beliefs to others. The difference between success and failure, happiness and sadness, wealth and poverty, the difference in how your children's lives turn out, the difference in whom you have as a mate, what you wear, what you drive, where you go, as well as your ultimate level of freedom and independence in life, comes down to one skill – your ability to sell yourself to yourself and to other people. And the selling skills that I will share with you in this book are incredibly simple to understand and to use every day in all your interactions.

For the past five years, I have been researching the world's top persuaders, marketers and salespeople. I have discovered how they consistently achieve their outstanding results; what sets them apart from the crowd; what makes them so successful; what makes them different. This book is my opportunity to share my findings with you. It is designed to help you implement the techniques and strategies that I have modelled from champion salespeople, marketers and persuaders.

Even if you are already a seasoned sales professional, I know you will find the wealth of brand-new ideas and tools to become even more successful right now thrilling! Obviously, I will also cover the fundamental selling tools, but even this ground will be covered in a new, enlightening way. Most of all, I will show you how to sell to others in an elegant, mutually nourishing way. I will show you not just how to make a sale, but how to make relationships that grow and become more valuable with time.

This book is designed to help you coach yourself to become more successful. Everyone needs a coach to help them to utilize resources they already have. You might not even be aware of your own resources right now. My wish for you is that you will experience the same extraordinary rush of self-discovery as I did when I was first exposed to the breakthrough techniques and strategies I am going to share with you.

You might think I'm making some pretty big claims. I would therefore like to share a little of my life and why I believe I can back up these claims I am making to you.

Nine years ago, I was one of the most successful advertising executives in the world. I held senior positions in the best advertising agencies in both South Africa and Canada. I could sell almost anything to almost anybody. Even though I didn't have the knowledge I now have, I was a 'natural' salesperson. However, I had one massive liability: I wasn't sold on myself. Although I knew how to get other people to buy, I had enormous doubts about *me myself*. That's why I was an accident waiting to happen. If you are not your own biggest fan; if you are not your own biggest customer; if you are not constantly reminding yourself how good you really are; if you are not constantly romancing yourself, you will eventually fail. That's a promise. As sure as the sun always rises in the east, failure follows self-doubt. I know. I hold a triple Master's degree in failure, burn-out and depression.

The more successful I became, the more I doubted my ability to sustain my level of performance. Have you ever noticed how success often brings you even more stress? The more you do, the higher other people's expectations become of you. You find yourself under greater and greater pressure to perform. Your fear of failure escalates until almost every waking or working moment is spent in fear and anxiety. That's what happened to me. In 1989, after eight years of meteoric success, I plunged into the nightmare world of acute depression. What really happened was that I gave in to my growing self-doubt, which eventually consumed me completely.

I was hospitalized, medicated and eventually treated with electroconvulsive therapy. On 28 February 1992 I emerged from my depression. I resolved never to doubt myself again. I also resolved never to take anything for granted again and to help others do the same. I committed myself to becoming the best 'sharer' of experience and insight I could be. I committed myself to the journey called *life*. I resolved never to insult myself or anyone else ever again. Most importantly, I committed myself to do whatever I had to do to learn and grow better, stronger and faster every day. If you haven't yet made that commitment, put this book down and don't continue until you make that vow to yourself.

The single biggest thing that has impressed me over and over again as I researched the top salespeople and persuaders in South Africa and the rest of the world, is that **the champions constantly do what other people are afraid or unwilling to do.** They know what to do and they do what they know. They are action oriented. Whatever it took, they did the necessary things that allowed them to produce the results they most desired in their lives. They were committed to their commitment.

Today, I am living the life of my dreams. I have my own highly successful marketing and motivation company; I have written three national best-selling books (I know this will be best-seller number four); all over the world, I work with companies to inspire, enthuse and energize their people; I have a happy family life; I am physically fitter than I have ever been; I have hundreds of fantastic friends and I am financially independent.

I am not telling you these things to impress you. I am not boasting about my achievements. The reason why I am sharing them with you is to impress upon you the fact that anything is possible when you master the art of effective selling. Everything and anything is available to you if you can learn to persuade people to believe in you by meeting their highest needs and truly being a giver of value.

I invite you to commit yourself one hundred per cent to mastering the techniques, strategies and ideas in this book. Read the book. Respond to the challenges I put to you. Then return again and again to those parts that you feel can benefit you the most. Practise what you have learnt as often as you can. Experiment, experiment, experiment. And share your knowledge with others.

Act on what you read and what you've learnt. The dictionary defines 'power' as 'the ability to act'. Almost all of us know what to do to be successful. The more I live my life, the more I realize just how simple it all is. However, while almost all of us know what to do, very few of us do what we know. Are you one of the many who merely know, or are you one of the few who do what they know? Decide!

I have called this book *Abracadabra!* because the best of the master persuaders are really magicians. They have an 'extraordinary or irresistible charm, influence or power'. They are 'mysteriously enchanting'. What's more, they spread their magic around. They sprinkle their magic dust wherever they go. They are not just out to enrich themselves through others – they are out to enrich others in order to enrich themselves. That's the real reason for this book. I want you to experience the joy and fulfilment that comes with truly influencing others. I know that you have the power to become an 'Abracadabran', a Master Persuader. You just have to let it out and let it shine.

You know what? If you have purchased this book, if you have laid out your hard-earned cash to explore the secrets of persuasion, selling and personal power contained in these pages, you already have a Champion attitude and you're probably already a Champion Salesperson. But no matter how good you may be, you are always looking for ways to get better. You are one of those special people who are on a permanent growth course.

However, I also know that as a Champion, you sometimes get frustrated because you can't always find the right kind of cutting-edge technology that you know you need to take yourself to the next level. That is why I wrote this book: to give you the edge you've been looking for to motivate and persuade both yourself and the people around you.

One day I hope to get a letter from you telling me how much this book has helped you to achieve your ultimate dreams and desires. When you're ready, write to me: Mike Lipkin, PO Box 41882, Craighall, 2024, Johannesburg, South Africa.

Right now, it is time to get going. I promise you that you will enjoy yourself as you dance your way through this book. I have written it in an easy-to-read, light-hearted style. Take it slowly or take it fast, but take it. Are you ready? Are you committed? Let's begin …

A foundation for success

Session One

The commitment to being a Champion Salesperson

Are you a zero-excuse kind of person?

Have you ever tried to make changes in your life and then failed? Have you attempted to make things happen and then not followed through? Have you learnt a new skill and then not applied it? Have you invested money in the past in learning a new skill and then not applied it? Have you ever not been able to produce the results you wanted despite your best efforts? Why not? What's held you back? Why did you not follow through?

The answer, I believe, is that you were 'interested' in getting results but you were not absolutely 'committed'. There is a huge difference between 'interest' and 'commitment'. When you are merely interested in making something happen, your inner dialogue sounds something like this: 'It would be nice if this happens. It would be *lekker*. I would like to do it. I wish I could do it.'

However, you have not fully invested yourself in the desired outcome. It remains something that may or may not happen. In your own mind, you haven't truly decided to go all the way for what you are 'interested' in. You've allowed for excuses and escape routes. For example, if you are just interested in jogging every day and you wake up one morning and you see it's raining, what do you do? You say to yourself, 'What a pity about the weather. I can't jog in these conditions.' And you go back to sleep. But if you are committed to jogging every day, you put on a raincoat and you get out there and you jog.

You become a zero-excuse kind of person.

If you're just interested, you're weak; if you're committed, you're strong

Over the past year, I have spoken to almost 100 000 people from Cape Town to Cairo to Canada. The central theme of my talks is that if you truly desire a result that is ambitious but realistic; if you have focus and discipline; if you are willing to pay the price of success and if you are fully committed to achieving your ambition, you will not be denied your dream. Many people approach me and tell me that life is not so simple. They tell me that they have tried 'everything' without getting the desired results. Everything? Have you noticed how we may try a couple of things that don't work and then we give up, saying, 'Nothing we do ever seems to work!' Or one or two people let us down and we say, 'People are so unreliable!' Or just as things seem to be going well, something minor misfires and you hear people lament, 'Life's a bitch and then you die.'

I believe: 'Life's a pitch and then you buy – from me!' Those who blame life and other people for their own shortcomings and failures have allowed themselves to be polluted by fear, uncertainty and doubt. They have become bitter, not better. They are focusing on reasons why things cannot be done and not on reasons to go where no one has ever been before.

What kind of person are you? The mere fact that you've purchased this book and that you've got this far, means that you're an explorer. But to truly succeed, you need to be an explorer who burns your bridges behind you. The moment you give yourself an escape route, you will be tempted to take it. Have you noticed how brilliant we all are at finding excuses why things cannot be done? Don't give yourself a reason to give up. People who make things happen find a way or make a way, often against all odds. One of the reasons why I'm so delighted to be living in South Africa right now is that the new champions are making things happen despite their lack of education or resources. They haven't been conditioned to believe that 'it cannot be done'. So they do it. They don't believe in failure and therefore they don't suffer from it. In other words, they are committed.

In the introduction, I shared with you my commitment to personal growth. As a result of this growth, I have eliminated doubt from my life. I believe that doubt is like a hole in the bucketful of confidence: if there is even a tiny hole, all the water eventually runs out.

I'd like to share a story with you. In July 1997, I was invited by the massive financial services company Deloitte & Touche to deliver a full-day workshop to their practice in Chicago. I was commissioned to address their 250 top people at a resort near the city. It was my first professional speaking engagement on American soil. What's more, I had an enormous amount riding on my performance. If I did well, I knew that there would be many more assignments. If I screwed up, I would be history. The night before my presentation, I had a full-blown panic attack – something I had not experienced for almost six years. I found myself focusing on how tough the assignment was. I began to doubt my ability to persuade and influence highly sophisticated and educated people.

I knew I had to recapture my confidence or my anxiety would reveal itself to my audience the following morning. I went back to my hotel room and hugged my fear. I asked myself why I was feeling so anxious. I told myself it was normal to feel tension on the eve of my most important presentation ever. I then consciously focused on all the big presentations I had delivered in the past year that had gone extremely well. I compared my current situation to my previous situations. Then I transferred my previous successes to my presentation the following morning. I concentrated on my vision of a spectacular success. I alchemized my doubt into power. The end result was that my performance exceeded both my expectations and those of the client. I received many more assignments from Deloitte & Touche – because I consciously eliminated doubt from my mind.

I guarantee that as long as you have even a shred of doubt about the course of action you're taking, you will always be acting from a position of weakness. When the going gets really tough, you'll turn back. Commitment is strength. It is concentration. It is focus. Ultimately, it is love, because without commitment, you cannot truly give yourself totally to anything.

Commitment is the common denominator of Champions

Commitment is the common denominator of champions, whether they are playing in the corporate, personal or sports arena. It is their self-granted permission to make the sacrifices and pay the price needed to consistently perform at their personal best. Without commitment, you can never be a compelling champion, merely a competent amateur. Have I convinced you about the power of commitment? Are you absolutely committed to being the best salesperson you can be? Are you advancing without self-doubt and reservation? Do you truly believe you can massively increase your power of persuasion? Are you excited about the prospect of making your goals a reality and helping others do the same? Are you revved? Are you juiced? If not, use these five steps to get your motor running:

1 **Get an image in your mind of who you want to be.** This evening, tomorrow, next week, next year – what kind of person do you want to be? Write down all your thoughts. Decide who and how you want to be and rehearse the future *you*. Have fun!

2 **Get an image in your mind of how you want other people to perceive you.** What role are you going to play in their success? What are other people looking for in the people with whom they decide to associate? What are their deepest needs?

3 **Love the other person in advance.** Focus on the characteristics that make the other person magical. Go for their magic, not their tragic.

4 **Rehearse your desired outcome before it happens.** Use the power of your imagination to visualize the achievements of your desired results. Then let the power of your subconscious boost your performance.

5   **Relax: whatever happens, life will go on.** You can only be at your best when you're operating from a place of inner calmness. Relax. Whatever happens, there will always be another chance. Believe that there are no failures, but only opportunities to learn.

Make a copy of this page and keep it with you. Get into the ritual of going through these five steps before you try to persuade anybody to do anything. Give it to your colleagues and customers. It's okay – my definition of 'copyright' is 'the right to copy'. Remember that true learning comes from:

1   **Desire:** Really, really want it. Act with head and heart.

2   **Focus:** Have a clearly defined target. Without a clear personal vision, you have double vision. If you don't know where you're going, how can you get there?

3   **Repetition:** Practise, practise, practise – but practise with high awareness. Avoid your automatic pilot.

4   **Integration:** Programme your mind to win. Develop empowering habits. Stand guard at the door of your mind.

5   **Reinforcement:** Consciously reinforce your outstanding behaviour. Catch yourself doing things right. That's why I shave my head: it feels good when I stroke myself. Recognize yourself – no one else will give you the recognition you feel you deserve. Recognition is like money – you can never get enough of it.

6   **Sharing:** The more you give, the more you get. The secret to living is giving. Give away whatever you want most. It will come back to you with interest.

How outstanding salespeople keep performing: the power of purpose, values and beliefs

I have discovered that the fundamental difference between outstanding salespeople and the merely adequate is that outstanding salespeople have purpose, values and beliefs to sustain them when the marketplace or life occasionally turns against them.

The power of purpose (or: purpose is power)

If you're not tapping your full potential as a Master Persuader or salesperson, it doesn't mean that you're short on talent and it may not even mean that you're not trying hard enough. It probably means that you have impotent goals or reasons to do what you are doing. After studying thousands of salespeople over the past five years, I have found that struggling salespeople simply do not have compelling enough reasons to perform or utilize all their resources.

I believe that 80 per cent of success in selling and persuading others comes from having a big enough WHY. Only 20 per cent of effective selling is knowing HOW.

The WHY comes first; the HOW comes second. As the renowned Austrian psychiatrist Victor Frankl said, 'If you have a big enough WHY, you can find any HOW.'

So the Number One quality of champion salespeople is that they are compelled to be the best because they have the WHY to be the best. This WHY is not only what they can achieve for themselves; it is also the value that they deliver to other people.

Salespeople who are not obsessed with the value they deliver to others can never sustain their high performance over the long term. Self-centred or selfish salespeople may be able to fool some of the people some of the time, but eventually they are found out. And when they are, rotten word-of-mouth ruins their reputation very rapidly.

The foundational law of effective selling is to really want to give the other person what *they* really want and to thoroughly enjoy the process. Have you ever noticed how you can tell instantly whether someone who is trying to sell you something actually cares about you as a person? There is a look in their eyes, a concern in their voice, a smile in their manner, an attractiveness in their aura. On the other hand, how do you feel about someone who is acting out of selfishness, who merely sees you as the ticket to his commission or, even worse, a hassle to be endured as part of their job? Remember: ***People don't care how much you know until they know how much you care.***

If your primary purpose is not to increase the quality of life or the performance of the people around you, treat these words as a *vuka* – a wake-up call. The most powerful technique in the world cannot compensate for the lack of desire to do good for others. ***It is the paradox of selling: If you care more for others than yourself, you will do what's best for yourself.***

What drugs are you on?

Over the past year, I delivered almost 300 talks and workshops. Every single talk I give has to be the best talk I have ever given. Every single talk has to be delivered with the same electrifying charge of energy and excitement. In my full-day or two-day programmes, I have to sustain the pace for eight to 16 hours. People often come up to me and ask, 'How do you keep it up? In fact, what drugs are you on? We want some!' The truth is that I do get exhausted. There are some days when the fatigue is so great that getting myself psyched for the session ahead is an almost impossible challenge. However, whenever I feel myself being sucked down into self-pity, I focus on WHY I am really doing what I am doing. I focus on getting people excited, on empowering them to go out and change their worlds.

'Yeah, right,' I can almost hear you say (hundreds of people have said it to me), 'Don't talk shit, you're doing it for the money.' I don't deny it. I am not Mother Teresa. But money is the bench-mark. It is a way of keeping score. It is also the passport to freedom and independence. It is not what drives me. This is one of the most important points I want to make: *Do it for love and the well-being of others and the money will follow. Do it for the money and you will fail!*

Your purpose is like your rudder. If you are steering yourself with the wrong purpose, you will end up on the rocks.

I have trained my mind to consider each talk as my very first one. I have trained myself to experience the thrill and the terror that accompanied my very first talk. That way, I never get complacent and I never get stale. No matter what state I am in, ten minutes before the talk I get myself pumped by focusing on one unquestionable truth: the people I am about to address don't know and don't care how many talks I've given before the one they are about to hear. They will judge my ability by the way I perform in the hours that I'm in front of them. My entire career rides on every single session. Does yours?

Make your purpose dramatically motivating!

Having the right, interdependent purpose is just the first step to becoming a Champion Salesperson. You have to describe your purpose to yourself in such a way that it inspires you. You have to become your own hero. You cannot give what you haven't got. If you don't turn yourself on, how are you going to turn anybody else on?

That's why my single-minded purpose is *To excite people into action*. A friend of mine who works as a financial adviser has a purpose which he describes as *To protect widows and orphans*. Walt Disney's purpose was *To create happiness*. My friend Reg Lascaris describes his purpose as *To provide people with the optimism and confidence to make the impossible possible*. My friend Dennis Regan, who is a personal trainer, has a purpose *To sculpt people's bodies into masterpieces*. Mother Teresa described her purpose as *To help people die with dignity*. Tom Peters, the well-known management consultant and author, describes his purpose simply as *The pursuit of 'Wow'*.

What is *your* purpose? How have you described it to yourself? Have you written it down? Does it inspire you? When you share it with others, does it inspire them to want to do business with you? If not, what are you waiting for? Begin formulating one right now. Have some fun. Loosen up. Make sure you're incandescent! Make sure people are drawn to your warmth! Make sure your flame sparks a fire in others.

Values: the hidden persuaders that guide our every decision and action

Two thousand years ago, the Oracle of Delphi gave humankind the following mandate: *Know Thyself!* The Old Testament commands us to 'treat thy neighbour as thyself'. Shakespeare advised us, 'Be true to thine own self for then thou canst not then be false to any man.' But despite these words of wisdom through the ages, the vast majority of the people I encounter every day haven't got a clue what their values are. They have never even looked inside themselves – partially out of ignorance, partially out of fear, partially because they cannot see the value in doing so. That's why there are so few salespeople who sustain championship levels of performance over the long term. So few of us have taken the time to understand what really makes us tick. No one else can tell you who you are on the inside. So go within and find yourself.

The most powerful human need is the need for security: the need to feel safe and free of fear. But many of us make the mistake of looking for security outside of ourselves. We look to the government, we look to relatives, we look to our employers, we look to our friends, we look to our spouses. But the only place where you will find genuine security is inside yourself. And the path to genuine security and strength is total understanding of your values.

Do you know what your values are? Do you know what guides the way you feel about anything? Could you tell me right now what your top eight values are, ranked in order of priority? If you can't, you're flying blind. You're making vital decisions unconsciously. I know that if you are the kind of person who not only bought this book but is actually reading it, you are already a star performer. Imagine how awesome you would be if you actually knew why you are doing what you are doing.

Six years after my recovery from my almost fatal bout of clinical depression, I now know that it was ignorance of my values that lead to my wrestling match with the demons. I was acting out of alignment with who I really was. I was not acting with integrity. My definition of integrity is simply 'being true to you'. When you consistently defraud yourself by not feeding your true values, emotional *snot en trane* is the result. It took me almost three years of agony to discover my values. You can do it simply by reading and applying the contents of this book.

Today, my golden rule is to act in total alignment with my values. Whenever I'm in doubt, I turn to my values for guidance. They are my inner leaders. And whenever I disobey them, I pay for it later. So I am now intimately familiar with my core values. They are: courage, health, growth, contribution, love, freedom, passion and making a difference. That's why I now make decisions very quickly and I change them slowly. I also almost never make decisions that I regret.

Obviously, I don't always get the results I desire. Obviously, I still have moments of self-doubt, anxiety and uncertainty. But they are rare and they are short-lived.

The five steps to value discovery

How can you decide what your values are? Answering and following these five steps will help you:

1 What gives you the most pleasure in life? What do you love doing the most? What really turns you on (other than the obvious thing)? What are you great at? What could you be great at? Write down as many responses as possible.

2 What do you fear most in life? What will you do almost anything to avoid?

3 In terms of your response to the first two questions, which elements are empowering and which are disempowering? For example, if you love people but you are scared of confrontation, you have a value called 'acceptance'. You need to be careful that this value does not inhibit you

from doing the right thing because you are scared of going up against someone who disagrees with you.

4 Now prioritize all your positive stimuli according to the benefit they deliver to you. Make sure that you are aware of any negative stimuli as identified in 2 that could sabotage your effectiveness.

5 Come back to your list of values again and again until you are certain these are your genuine values. Test them on the streets of life.

Beliefs: the Abracadabra of sales effectiveness

Whatever we believe, we make true. Beliefs are our internal truths. They are the way we look at the world. If you're a pessimist, you see a future that's about to go wrong. You will take appropriate action and, more than likely, you'll become a prophet. Things will go wrong, you will get depressed, you will say, 'I told you so!'

Whether you believe you can or you can't do something, you're right!

All a belief really is, is a feeling of certainty. Beliefs are the reality between our ears. So, for example, if you believe that people are dishonest and uncaring, that's what you'll see when you meet them. However, if you believe that people are essentially good, kind and giving if given half a chance, that's what you'll see when you meet them. And that's what they will see when they meet you.

Have you ever noticed how you can tell instantly if someone is delighted to see you or not? Have you noticed how you feel an instant rapport or you don't? Can you sense the other person's acceptance or rejection of you straight away? Do you reciprocate feelings of friendliness and caring with the same feelings of friendliness and caring? Do you respond with anger and rejection to anger and rejection? You see, life is a mirror that reflects back at us what we are.

There is an old Zen tale about a traveller walking from the village in the valley to the village in the mountains. He comes across a monk walking in the opposite direction. He asks the monk what kind of people live in the village in the mountains. In return, the monk asks him what kind of people live in the village in the valley. The traveller replies that they are unfriendly, selfish and inhospitable. 'In that case,' said the monk, 'I expect you will find exactly the same kind of people in the mountains.'

I believe it is not people's ability that makes them successful; it is their beliefs about their ability. In all the sales and motivational sessions I deliver, I always ask delegates a simple question: 'What is the one most important thing that you would like to learn, change or improve to be the best you can be?' In almost every instance, their immediate response is: 'Confidence: the ability to act or say whatever I want to say or do irrespective of place or audience.'

When I ask people what is standing between them and this confidence they desire, they respond: 'Fear, specifically the fear of making a fool of myself in front of others.' It seems that fear of humiliation ranks just below fear of death as a source of terror.

After connecting with hundreds of thousands of people across the world over the past five years, I believe that this thing called IQ is greatly overrated. I have met so-called highly intelligent people who are struggling. And I have met people who are not intellectually gifted who are flying. The Abracadabra of personal power is simply their beliefs about what they're capable of doing.

Your life will change when you change your beliefs about your life. Sometimes, the smarter we are, the more we focus on all the things that can go wrong; the more we dwell on our weaknesses and inadequacies; the more we criticize other people; the more we search for all that's screwed up in the world.

Beliefs are like taps in your brain. Negative beliefs will turn off the tap of power, energy and commitment. Empowering beliefs will turn those magical taps on full-blast. It's your call. Many people refuse to turn on their taps because they are scared of success. They are scared that maybe they will not be able to handle the pressure that comes from being a champion. They are scared of giving it their all. They are fearful that maybe they won't be able to handle their increased velocity. Are you?

Your beliefs are the ultimate reason why you will win or fail the game of life

We become the image we have of ourselves. In other words, we become the person we believe we really are. What do you believe about yourself? What is your identity? How do you define yourself? What makes you unique? Why should I want to associate with you?

What do you believe about life and other people? Do your beliefs make you stronger? Do your beliefs fill you with optimism and joy? Or do your beliefs weigh you down like lead shoes? Do you even know what you believe in?

I would like to share with you my beliefs about myself, life, other people and the world around me:

My identity (what I believe about myself)

'I am the most effective and passionate sales and persuasion coach in the country. I am a force for personal and interpersonal good. I am outrageous, response-able, courageous, passionate, compassionate, exciting, bold, proactive and uplifting. I am a person who helps others to let their own light shine.'

My beliefs about life, other people and the world around me

'I am here to make a difference by learning, growing and passionately sharing. Life is a gift. People are miracles. The deeper my friendships, the more joy and success I experience. If I meet people's true needs with total sincerity and commitment to serve, they will consistently do business with me. My work is pure magic. I am blessed. I am the luckiest person I know. The secret to living is giving. I am guided. Everything that happens to me serves me. No matter how good things are right now, they can only get better. No matter how good I am right now, I can only get better.'

Most of us, though, haven't taken time out to focus on our beliefs, to strengthen what serves us and to discard what doesn't. I am here to share this with you: *Your beliefs are the ultimate reason why you will win the game of life or why you will fail it. They are your most powerful resources when you find yourself walking through the valley of the shadow of death as we all will at some time or another.*

My friend Reg Lascaris has a wonderful saying: Friends may come and go but enemies keep accumulating! Anytime you try something bold, there will be people trying to bring you down. There will be people telling you why it will never work or why it's impossible. If you allow their doubts to corrupt your commitment, you will lose your personal power. Your beliefs are your inspiration and protection against the forces of doubt and uncertainty.

The beliefs of Champion Salespeople

Champion Salespeople never believe in failure. In fact, they believe that FAIL really stands for First Action In Learning.

- ☛ They always overestimate their ability.
- ☛ They believe that they are never personally rejected by others; every now and then they simply meet someone who can't appreciate the quality of their service.
- ☛ They believe in possibility.

- ☞ They believe that a massive sale lies just around the corner.
- ☞ They believe that every day they mine another layer of their limitless potential.
- ☞ They believe that they are gifted and that other people are lucky to be around them.
- ☞ They believe that they are there to make others happy and fulfilled.
- ☞ They believe that people are inherently good and worthy of their trust.
- ☞ They believe that everything that happens to them serves them.
- ☞ They believe that they are a resource to their customers; not just a seller.
- ☞ They believe that they are the most valuable people in their customers' lives.

Do it now: harness the power of belief

Take time out right now to pin-point your personal identity and your core beliefs about people and the world around you. Then share your beliefs with others. The next time you are with a prospect, tell her what you believe about life. *Moenie skaam wees nie.* You know, my most satisfying moments are when someone who has attended one of my programmes comes up to me and tells me how much more powerful they are because they not only decided to pin-point their beliefs but also to share them with others. They say how much they regret not doing it sooner. They tell me about how receptive other people are when they open up their minds and hearts to them. Because, above all else, people want to be treated like people. The more high-tech this world becomes, the more high-touch we need to be.

Harness the power of your beliefs. What are the ten (if not more) beliefs you have in your life that empower you as a person and a professional? These beliefs can be general beliefs, like 'I am …' or 'Life is …' or 'People are …' Or these beliefs can be rules, like 'If I do this, it means that …' or 'If people do this, then …' Write down these beliefs. Also write down the consequences of each belief. In my case, for example, I believe that everything that happens to me serves me. The consequence of this belief is that I view every experience as a learning experience. Even when the experience is a tough one, I have programmed my mind to ask a simple question: What can I learn from this? How can I use it? How can this experience make me stronger? How can I get better, not bitter?

Another personal example: I believe I am a person who helps others let their own light shine. The consequence of this belief is that I feel really good about what I've become and the impact I have on other people. I enjoy living one of my most important values: contribution. I know that other people enjoy having me around. I know that if I help others let their own light shine, my light will shine ever brighter.

The key questions you need to ask yourself are: What would I need to believe in order to be the kind of person I want to be? What do I need to believe to live my purpose? What are the beliefs that will help me squeeze the juice out of life? What are the beliefs that will help me love, honour and serve my fellow South Africans? What do I need to believe about myself and my ability to become a Master Persuader?

Go on an adventure inside your mind. Take some time and dedicate it to yourself. Go somewhere on your own. Go to your favourite place and treat yourself to thinking about yourself. The true essence of personal power is a quiet place inside yourself. A place that centres you no matter how chaotic the conditions around you become. Write down all the empowering beliefs you can think of and then write down the consequences of each belief as follows:

Empowering, powerful belief no. 1:

Consequences:

Empowering, powerful belief no. 2:

Consequences:

and so on.

Then ask yourself what additional beliefs you would need to have in order to take your life to a new level of success. Create at least another three beliefs and focus on them over the next few weeks until they become part of you.

Then ask yourself what additional beliefs you would need to have in order to become a Master Persuader. Create at least another three beliefs and focus on them over the following few weeks until they eventually become part of you.

The important thing is to keep experimenting with new beliefs. Life is a learn-as-you-go process. It's not what people can do that makes a difference, it's what they believe they can do that makes a difference. Beliefs can be chains or wings. You are the one who decides that.

Self-awareness: the Master Persuader's edge

As you involve yourself with the rest of this book, always carry this word with you: self-awareness. Have you ever done something without being aware that you were doing it? Have you ever said something that you've regretted? Have you ever thought about a situation you have found yourself in and said to yourself, 'If only I have said …'? Have you noticed that the more tired or pressurized you are, the less aware you are of your every word and action? Have you ever said something to someone else and found out later that the other person was somehow offended by what you said?

There is one thing that I've learnt and that I'd like to share with you: *Your ability to remain constantly aware of the impact you're having on the other person is what gives you the edge.*

I call my self-awareness the video-camera of my mind. As I travel around the world speaking to people in groups both large and small, I am constantly observing the impact I'm having on people through the video-camera of my mind. Especially towards the end of an eight-hour session I am particularly vigilant. If I see that people are tiring or becoming restless, I take appropriate action: I will either get them to move, tell a joke or give them a break.

Nothing is more frustrating or irritating to your customer or audience than being with someone who is not acutely sensitive to their needs and desires. From now on, tune in to the frequency of your audience and give them what they want to hear. Because if people don't like what you're saying or if they're bored by what you're saying, you may as well be talking to yourself.

Were you you?

The reason why I have invested so many words on the issues of purpose, values and beliefs is that without an intimate understanding of what these concepts are, you will always be wondering who *you* really are; whether what you are doing is really the right thing; how you are coming across to other people; whether they accept you or not. In other words, you will always be second- guessing yourself. You will be robbing yourself of the confidence and certainty that comes with inner knowledge, understanding and love.

Leo Buscalia, the American motivator known as the Doctor of Love, says that when we go up to meet our creator, she only asks us one question: 'Were you you?' Were you the best you you could be? Or were you trying to be someone else? Were you afraid to be you because of what other people would say? Did you honour the you that you were? Or did you spend your life getting down on yourself?

It's no coincidence that you've got this far in the book to read these words. If the only action you take as a result of buying this book is to make the decision to be you, your personal effectiveness will rocket.

What we're really all selling is nothing but a sense of certainty

At the end of the day, what we're really all selling is nothing but a sense of certainty. When other people sit across from you and listen to your sales pitch, your ideas, your opinions, your suggestions or your recommendations, what they're really evaluating is: Can I trust this person's judgement? If I buy into this person, will I get the results I desire? Does this person inspire me with confidence?

You cannot radiate certainty if you do not have it. All of us have built-in bullshit detectors. We can sense when someone is operating out of uncertainty – it gives off a bad smell. Remember that the first step to the inner, unshakeable confidence we all desire is the understanding, affection and passion for ourselves. In fact, I'm so committed to myself that I've become a legend in my own mind!!

The five commitments to being a Champion Salesperson

I am now asking you to make five commitments to becoming a Champion Salesperson. I am asking you to make a vow to the most important person in the world to you: yourself. If you honour and respect yourself, you will honour and respect others. If you let yourself down, you will do the same with others.

In the movie *Rob Roy,* Liam Neeson said these powerful words: *Honour is a gift a man gives to himself. It is something no other man can give him and it is something no other man can take away.*

If you want to become a Champion Salesperson, make these five commitments and honour them. Keep them close to you. Make them aloud. Declare them with passion and conviction. Make them again and again. Make them day after day. And, as always, help others do the same.

1   **I am absolutely committed to stretching myself beyond my past limits. I will take my most important 'shoulds' and make them my most important 'musts'. And if I must, I can. And if I can, I will!**

2   **I am committed to be totally responsible. I alone am responsible for my personal growth and development as a Champion Salesperson. I will absolutely maximize all my resources in order to become a Master Persuader. I know I have so much power inside me, it's scary. I will learn to access it and use it to promote the well-being of others.**

3 I am absolutely committed to being flexible. Flexibility creates choice
   and adaptability. I know that the person with the most flexibility is
   the dominant force in any interaction. I am smarter than the people
   who major in minor things, and who become stuck in the rigidity of
   their past.

4 I am absolutely committed to being a contributor to other people. I
   give them respect, love, knowledge and support. I focus on what I can
   give to others, not what I can get from others. I always, always give
   more than I take.

5 I am absolutely committed to living my life with consistent excitement and energy. I know I am only as good as the mood I am in. I
   know happiness is an inside job. I do not have to be successful to be
   excited; I have to be excited to be successful. I will consistently focus
   on those things that make me excited, especially when I am faced with
   massive challenges!

You now know your purpose, values and core empowering beliefs (if not,
at least you've begun the process of finding out what they are). You have
also made a massive commitment to being a Champion Salesperson. It's
time to start discovering the skills to use your purpose, values, beliefs and
commitments to get people to buy what you have to sell.

A foundation for success

The science of persuasion: why we buy

Session overview

Most salespeople believe that the selling process is all about making the customer buy their product or service. They often attempt to push the customer into making a decision that the customer is not completely comfortable with, in order to make the sale. These salespeople are out to make their figures through any means possible.

That approach may have worked in the past. In the current South Africa, however, we have a far more sophisticated consumer; a consumer who has more choices than ever before. This kind of consumer or customer cannot be pushed around. They won't respond to pressure applied from the outside. This kind of customer responds primarily to internal pressure in the form of desire. Once they have decided that they want and need a product or service, they will find ways to justify their purchase.

The purpose of this session is to share with you what really makes people buy. It focuses on their desires and how these desires are triggered.

As a result of successfully completing this session, you will be able to:
- ☛ describe what makes people really buy or do anything else in their lives. You will be able to utilize this knowledge to create deep and powerful motivation within prospects to desire your product or service.
- ☛ understand why a customer does not buy, which will, in turn, assist you in using those distinctions to make better sales presentations in the future.

You have to become the 'Wizard of Wants'

Remember: *80 per cent of the time, people buy on Wants; 20 per cent of the time, they buy on Needs.*

We often use the two concepts of Wants and Needs without understanding what they really mean, or what the essential, massive difference between them is.

I define a need as *an urgent necessity without which the consumer cannot function.* If your customer is starving or suffering from a deep thirst, food and water are needs. If your customer has a build-up of fluid in his system after an evening of partying and he has to go to the bathroom, he has an obvious need that has to be met. If I am staging a major public event to which I have to attract thousands of people, I have a need for the kind of advertising and promotion that will draw people to my programme. In designing the cover of this book, I had a need for someone who could deliver the striking, pick-me-up cover that encouraged you to buy the book.

I define a want as *a wish or craving for something that satisfies a customer's emotional drive*. Every time someone makes the decision to buy a product or service because of tastes, desires, self-image, status, recognition, aspirations or dreams, they are buying on wants.

If the economy were solely dependent on people buying goods and services because of their needs, we would be in a permanent depression. The whole world of business revolves around wants, not needs.

This means that the entire process of selling is dependent on your capacity to get your customers to want your product or service more than anything else.

You have to become the 'Wizard of Wants' if you aspire to become a Master Persuader and salesperson. Unless you have a monopoly on your customers' 'want' of your product or service, there are always going to be a gaggle of suppliers who can meet the customer's needs. There are lots and lots of 'competent' salespeople. If you are merely a 'competent' salesperson, you will survive in this country. I'm not sure how well you'll survive, but you'll get by.

However, if you're a compelling salesperson, if you are the Wizard of Wants, you will thrive! Being the Wizard of Wants, you have the ability to build tremendous 'want' for you and your product or service. Your customer will crave you and what you have to sell so intensely that they will find a way to justify buying from you, even if your price or product does not enjoy an advantage over the competition.

How would you like your customer to desire you and your product so strongly that they are blinded to the approaches of all your competitors? How would you like it if your customer had, in the words of that wonderful song, 'only eyes for you'?

Desire happens in a heartbeat

'You never get a second chance to make a first impression,' the old saying goes. Your prospect or customer makes a decision about you the moment you shake hands. Desire happens in a heartbeat. This is especially true if you are meeting someone for the first time, but it is also true with people who you have been working with for some time. Every conversation or meeting with another person is either an investment or a disinvestment in the relationship. Making investments in relationships is the most powerful thing you can do. Relationships are the only assets, outside of yourself, worth building.

The law of perception

Have you ever noticed how quickly we judge people? That's the main difference between us and God. God doesn't presume to judge us until the end of our days. We judge people on impact. Have you noticed how we seldom change our minds about people once we have judged them? Becoming a Master Persuader means becoming a master at managing people's perceptions of you. Because that's what we actually are: a perception in other people's minds.

Do you know how you want people to perceive you? If I asked you to write a personal ad for yourself that would create massive 'want' in your customers for your goods and services, could you do it? Do this right now. If you haven't done it before, it will probably be one of the toughest things you've ever done. Here's a tip: Write your personal ad in such a way that the customer associates you with the fulfilment of their most ardent desires. 'Position' yourself as the gateway to your customer's idea of success.

If you asked me to write my personal ad that would persuade you to want to come and listen to me, here's how I would craft it:

'If you want to get the results you really desire in your life and develop the absolute confidence that comes with being a powerful persuader, listen to Mike Lipkin. Over the past year, he has personally empowered over 100 000 people around the world. He is widely acknowledged as South Africa's most powerful motivator and sales coach. Listen to Mike and you will not only have the most fun you can have with your clothes on, you will become unstoppable.'

Pain and pleasure – the Siamese twins of human motivation

The twin forces of motivation behind all human behaviour are the desire to gain pleasure and the need to avoid pain. The master formula for persuasion is therefore: ***People have to associate buying from you with massive pleasure and not buying from you with immense pain.***

Notice that the formula says 'buying *from you*' – *who* people buy from is far more important than *what* they are buying. Ask yourself, 'Do all my customers and colleagues associate pleasure with dealing with me? Do they see me as an antidote to their pain? Will they feel a sense of loss or discomfort if they don't deal with me?'

Remember that people will do more to avoid pain than they ever will to get pleasure. Think about the pain that many people are going through in South Africa right now. Think about all the things that you worry about during the course of an average week. Whenever a country goes through the kind of social earthquake that we are going through, people experience extreme levels of anxiety, uncertainty and fear. There is one vital fact that you need to make your own, namely: *Your customers or personal stakeholders must see you as their resource against fear and doubt. You must become a walking security blanket. You must be your customer's one absolute constant in a world of violent change.*

Champion Salespeople go beyond selling benefits. They sell consequences. Traditional sales training teaches that we should sell the benefits that our product offers customers, not the features of our product. But in order to become a Champion Salesperson, you have to sell consequences that go far deeper than mere product performance.

The seven vital questions

Just like you, your prospects have seven vital questions that they ask themselves either consciously or subconsciously:

1 **Do you really have my best interests in mind?**
2 **Can I really trust you?**
3 **What's in it for me?**
4 **What do I have to give up in order to buy your product?**
5 **What's the risk to me if I make the wrong decision?**
6 **What will other people think of me if I buy this?**
7 **What should I do?**

Ask yourself how your prospect would respond to these seven questions when it comes to dealing with you. Unless you score off the charts on the positive consequences to the customer, you can never hit championship level. If someone gets a negative reading on any of the seven vital questions, it means they associate pain with buying from you. If they get positive readings, it means that they either associate pleasure with buying from you, or that they associate pain with not buying from you.

How to give people pleasure by stirring up their pain

People sometimes call me when they have already decided to use me and just want to find out whether I'm available. However, I often have to motivate people to use my services or buy my books even when they don't think they have a need for my services or books. In those instances, I motivate people to buy from me by getting them to the point where they are dissatisfied with the way things are. Sound intriguing? Then read on about the steps I follow:

1 **Find a person's pain.** Understand what the person is really missing. What do they lack in their lives? What's bugging them emotionally? The first step in selling is to find out enough about the customer in order to really appreciate their problem, their hurt, their emotional thorn in the side.

2 **Disturb them.** As cruel as this sounds, we need to stir up their pain. We need to get them to focus on what they're missing. I guarantee you that if someone is feeling pain, they are motivated. If they are comfortable with the way things are, selling to them will be like pushing water up-hill. An undisturbed prospect will not buy.

3 **Heal them.** We need to heal their pain by offering them a new set of choices, usually in the form of our product or service. And we need to demonstrate how our product or service will take their pain away.

Remember this fundamental selling truth: *People make decisions based on emotional reasons. They justify their decisions based on logical reasons.*

We all need to appear rational to ourselves and to other people. Have you ever met anyone who admitted they did things for emotional reasons? No way! Not us! We're all extremely rational, wise and well-balanced. Yeah, right! And pigs can fly.

To illustrate my point, I'll share this story with you: I have a friend who just bought himself a new car, a BMW 750i to be exact. He paid almost R500 000 for this car. When I asked him why he bought the car, his response was, 'Because it's durable! It's also very safe, reliable and it's got a great resale value.'

I looked at him in disbelief, but he refused to acknowledge the real reason why he bought the car. Then we indulged our mutual passion for single malt scotch whisky together. Finally, after a couple of stiff drinks, he turned to me and asked, 'Hey, Mike, do you really want to know why I bought that car?'

'Of course,' I responded, smiling. 'Because it's me,' he said proudly, 'I don't drive that car – I *wear* it!'

Makes you think, doesn't it? Of course, you would never buy a car for such emotional reasons! I understand that. But we need to appreciate the fact that other people might.

In order to sell, you need to manage the customer's ERBN, LRBN and DRAB

Imagine a see-saw. Place two rocks on the one side. Place another load on the other side. The see-saw will obviously settle on the side of the heavier load. It's the same with selling. On the one side of the customer's mental see-saw, there are two rocks: their ERBN and LRBN. On the other side is their DRAB.

ERBN stands for Emotional Reasons to Buy Now.

LRBN stands for Logical Reasons to Buy Now.

DRAB stands for Dominant Reason to Avoid Buying.

Get someone to buy from you by loading up their ERBN. Stir their pain. Heal their pain. Get them to associate pleasure with you.

Ensure further that you provide them with LRBN. They need to justify their purchase decision to themselves and others.

Understand, address and minimize their DRAB. This is essential, so that they can eliminate their own barriers to purchasing from you.

ERBN are extremely relevant when it comes to selling commercial products or services. It is a myth that we become more rational when buying on behalf of our companies. If anything, we become even more emotional because there may be more at stake.

Remember this fundamental selling truth: *In a world where products and services are increasingly the same, a powerful emotional appeal is the way to own the high ground in your prospect's mind. Others may be able to copy your product or service, but they can never copy the emotions you generate in your customer's heart.*

Let me give you a personal example of how I recently handled a prospect's ERBN, LRBN and DRAB. I staged a major public event in Johannesburg: a full-day seminar with an admission price of almost R800 per person. I had a list of prospects whom I approached to attend the session. One specific prospect was the sales director of a large financial services company. He had a sales force of 50 people. If he brought all his people to the session, it would be a major coup for me, not to mention a major financial bonus.

I had done my homework on the prospect prior to the meeting, but I hadn't pin-pointed his specific problem or hurt. What's more, despite my articulate presentation, I didn't manage to provide the client with a major emotional reason to attend or to bring his people to the programme. So I probed for his hurt. I asked him what he believed was the biggest challenge facing his people. What did he believe was holding his people back? What was their greatest obstacle to success? I asked him how their frustrations made them feel about him as their leader. I asked him about how they responded to him when he criticized them for not achieving the targets he had set. Finally, after identifying him as someone who cared deeply for his people, I helped him heal the hurt by asking him how he would feel if his people became grateful to him for giving them the opportunity to grow by attending my seminar. I asked him how he would feel when his people overcame their frustrations because of his investment in their performance and growth. He smiled and nodded his head. But just as I thought I had made the sale, he told me he didn't have R40 000 to send them (50 x R800). I isolated budget as the sole DRAB by saying, 'If budget were not a problem, would you send your people?' 'Definitely,' he replied. 'How much could you afford?' I asked him. 'R25 000,' was his reply. 'Why don't we meet half-way?' I responded. 'I promise you that your investment of R32 500 will turn each salesperson into a sales force. I promise you their productivity and happiness will soar. And they'll thank you for it. Think about how great that will make you feel!' Needless to say, he sent his people. What's more, on a group of 50 people, I would have offered him a discount of 20 per cent anyway!

Time for some self-exploration to ensure you really understand and exploit the power of ERBN, LRBN and DRAB

Take a little time to consider the following:
- ☛ Think about three important purchases you have made recently (personally or on behalf of the business). How big was your want? What made you really want to buy? Was it emotion or logic that made you buy? How did you justify it?
- ☛ Remember a time when you had a strong desire to buy and you still didn't buy. Think of three situations. Did you have Dominant Reasons to Avoid Buying?
- ☛ Think about a recent sale that you made to someone. What made them buy? Was it their ERBN or LRBN? How did you deal with their DRAB?
- ☛ Think about a recent sale that you didn't make. What was your prospect's DRAB? What ERBN and LRBN did you offer them to make the sale? Why were they not strong enough? How would you do it differently after participating in this session?

A foundation for success

Session Three
The seven master tools of persuasion

It's not *what* you say, it's *how* you say it that persuades people to buy into you. Be self-aware!

There are many theories in the field of selling about what really influences or persuades people to buy. Most sales training programmes focus on what to say in order to persuade the prospect. However, only seven per cent of your ability to connect with people is the actual words you use: 38 per cent of what influences them is the tonality or quality of your voice and 55 per cent of what influences them is the way you use your body: your posture, your breathing pattern, your facial expressions, and all other forms of body language.

From now on, remember the most important words in the art of persuasion: *Be self-aware.* No matter what the circumstance or the challenge, be aware of your impact on the other person. Be aware of the level of energy in your voice and your body language. Be aware of *their* responses to you. Watch their body language. Listen to the tone of their voice. Remember: *The physical and emotional state that you are in when you are with a client says more to them than any words you will ever use.*

The purpose of this session is to share with you the most important tools of persuasion available. It will broaden your view of the persuasion process to such an extent that you can consistently utilize more of your skills to achieve the results you desire and deserve.

As a result of successfully completing this session, you will be able to:

☞ describe and use the seven most powerful tools of persuasion. These approaches can be used together or separately, depending on your particular challenge.

☞ design and plan a series of effective strategies that will give you confidence in meeting any client's needs and wants.

The first master tool of persuasion: *rapport*

The vital ingredient of every successful relationship is the magic of rapport. Rapport is when two or more people connect with each other in a harmonious, mutually trusting and rewarding way. It's when you feel the other person really, really understands, empathizes with and respects you, what you stand for and how you feel. Rapport is when you thoroughly enjoy being with another person because you just know they are very similar to you in their values, their beliefs and their behaviour.

Think about it: Have you ever said to yourself, 'I like that person because we've got huge differences!'? On the other hand, how many times have you said, 'I like that person because we've got so much in common.'? Remember the fundamental law of rapport: *People like to be with people who are like they are or how they would like to be! Learn to chameleonize yourself!*

I have seen salespeople fail to sell on many occasions because they failed to build rapport. They just do not 'talk the other person's language'. They do not respect or integrate the other person's culture. As a result, they never bridge the gap that exists between strangers. An emotional bond is never fully established and the relationship, therefore, never becomes all that it can be.

In order to become a Champion Salesperson, you have to learn to chameleonize yourself. That means you have to adapt your personality, posture and language to that of the other person. And you have to do it instantly. It does not mean becoming hypocritical. It does not mean being insincere. It does not mean being who you are not. It does mean being versatile, being flexible and being able to change your 'packaging' according to circumstance, while your character and integrity stay constant.

Champion Salespeople do not apply the Golden Rule – they apply the Platinum Rule

Traditional thinking states that you should always practise the golden rule: Do unto others as you would have done unto you. But think about that statement carefully. If you practise the golden rule, you are assuming that other people want to be treated the same way that you want to be treated. Nothing could be further from the truth.

In fact, applying the golden rule is one of the biggest mistakes we all make. We assume our likes and dislikes are the other person's likes and dislikes. But everyone is different. We have different tastes, rules and preferences. So what's the solution?

The solution is Lipkin's Platinum Rule: *Do unto others as they would have done unto them.* In other words, don't treat people the way you want to be treated; treat them the way *they* want to be treated. Let's now explore how to do that.

Eight ways to build rapport (or apply the Platinum Rule) with prospects

1 **Mirror and match your prospect's posture and tone.** Imitate your prospect's posture and tone of voice in a subtle way. Don't be obvious in your strategy; simply ensure that you reflect your prospect's behaviour.

If your prospect talks fast, pick up your speech pace. If they talk softly, lower your own voice. If they talk loudly, raise your voice.

2 **Use the language your prospect speaks.** Listen to the words they use and build them into your vocabulary. Listen especially carefully to those words that the prospect uses when they are excited or happy. Here are some examples of the words I use when I want to build rapport with prospective clients:

When I am with clients in the restaurant or food industry, I use words like: 'I have a sizzling idea for you. I hope you have an appetite for something mouth-watering.'

When I am with clients in the automotive industry, I say: 'We need to overhaul our approach because we're not firing on all cylinders. This is where the rubber hits the road. So let's put the pedal to the metal and recharge our batteries.'

When I am with clients in the financial industry, I might say: 'We need to make more deposits into the emotional bank accounts of our clients. We've been withdrawing more than we've been depositing; that's why we're in emotional overdraft with them. The highest return on investment we can get is investment in relationships. So invest in me and I'll give you the highest return on investment of any investment you'll make this year and that's the bottom line.'

I also had this technique used on me to get me to take action I wasn't going to take. I received a call from someone in Cape Town who wanted me to help her launch a new product, but who didn't have much money to pay me. I began to turn her down. Then she said, 'All I want is a few minutes to tap into your energy.' Now that happens to be my favourite phrase. I believe that we are all just bundles of energy and that life is about tapping into your own and other people's energy. The moment she used those magic words, I was motivated to help her because I believed she was just like me. As it so happened, she told me later (after I had helped her) that we had a mutual friend who attended the same sales programmes as me. Her friend told her that if she used those words I would do whatever she wanted. And she was right. Practise this technique. It's very powerful.

3 **Pay your prospect a sincere compliment.** Find a reason to pay your prospect a sincere compliment, with the emphasis on the word 'sincere'. Your compliment can be on the performance of their company; their personal performance; their family; their products; their building; their

people; their culture, and so on. If you focus on the magic in the other person, they will focus on the magic in you. It's the law of reciprocation. But it must be sincere.

I find that this is one of the most difficult actions for South Africans to perform. We are so used to looking for the negative in people and situations that it is almost impossible for us to focus on what makes them magnificent. This anecdote illustrates this attitude perfectly: A visitor to the Cape West Coast came across a fisherman taking his lobsters to the market. The visitor was perplexed to see that the fisherman was carrying the lobsters in a very shallow tray. So he called to the fisherman, 'Mr Fisherman, shouldn't you put those lobsters in a deeper tray?' 'Nay,' replied the fisherman, 'these lobsters are South African lobsters. When one climbs up, five will pull him down.'

No matter how awkward it may feel, go out of your way to tell the people around you what it is you admire about them. Try to pay at least ten genuine compliments a day. Do a 'compliment audit' at the end of every day.

4 **Give your prospect a referral, especially from someone in their industry.** Giving your prospect a referral from someone in their industry accelerates the process of rapport enormously. A referral immediately allows you to tell your prospect how you managed to enhance the performance of a company confronted with similar challenges to those of your prospect. Remember that the prospect is always asking: Can I really trust this person even though I don't know him?

It is all about trust. Anything you can do right up front to get the prospect to feel that they can trust you will help you establish rapport.

The first lesson in prospecting that every salesperson learns is: When you have made a sale, get a referral. People trust those people they already know more than they trust those they don't know.

5 **Listen genuinely.** One of the most powerful ways to generate rapport is simply to listen with genuine interest to the customer. We all love to be with people who make us feel special. The most powerful way to make someone feel special is to listen to them intensely. By listening, I mean listening with your heart, your mind, your eyes, your entire self.

Reg Lascaris, chairman of the Hunt Lascaris TBWA advertising agency, is a master at this. He has the ability to become absolutely still as he single-mindedly focuses all his attention on the person speaking to him. It's as if he is saying, 'What you have to share with me is so important that I don't want to miss any of it. I am extremely interested in you.' Even Reg admits that it is his ability to listen that has been the biggest contributor to his phenomenal success.

Examine your own ability to listen. When people speak to you, do you find your mind wandering? Do you fiddle with things around you? Are you always trying to do something else while people are talking to you? Do you focus on making them feel special? Does your body language broadcast your interest or the lack of it? What kind of expression do you have on your face? Are you smiling slightly or is your mouth turned the wrong way round? Even when we're happy, most South Africans forget to tell their face! A mere smile will go a long way to putting a smile on someone else's face.

If all you do as a result of reading this book, is concentrate on your listening skills, you will find that your ability to sell will rocket. Start practising these skills now. Try listening like a Champion Salesperson to the very next person you meet, and see the difference it makes in how you relate.

Always make notes when a prospect is talking to you. Nothing communicates your interest and commitment more than actually writing down what the client is saying. Taking notes tells the client that you are going to review what he has said after the session. Taking notes also helps with your follow-up meetings and meeting reports.

6 **Bring up a subject of mutual interest.** If you are familiar with the customer's business, talk about key trends, developments and challenges. If you know the customer has certain personal interests that coincide with yours, raise them. The moment you begin to talk about mutual interests, you begin the process of rapport.

7 **Use humour.** This step should only be used by those individuals skilled in the art of making people laugh and smile. Nothing can be more powerful than the skilful use of humour, but nothing can be more damaging than inappropriate humour. Before you practise humour on important prospects, practise humour on people who will still love you if your humour bombs.

Some of my most ecstatic moments have been when I have used humour in a talk that has captured the imagination of the audience. For me there is no sweeter sound than tens or hundreds of people enjoying my humour. But I'll tell you this, some of my most embarrassing moments have been when my humour failed to connect, or worse still, when it alienated the audience. However, always remember the three most important words when it comes to personal growth and development as a Champion Salesperson: experiment, experiment, experiment.

8   **Understand your prospect's beliefs and values.** This is possibly the most important way to build rapport and apply the Platinum Rule. Unless you understand why your prospects do what they do, unless you know their most important beliefs and values, how can you truly connect with them? A very simple way of getting a sense of someone's beliefs and values is to ask them these two simple kinds of questions:
   ☛ *When it comes to ..., what is most important to you?* (The blank refers to whatever subject you're discussing.) When a prospect tells you what's most important to them, they are telling you about their beliefs and values.
   ☛ What has to happen for you to feel as though your expectations have been met? This question will help you to discover the prospect's rules for success and satisfaction.

We'll explore questions as a master tool of persuasion in greater depth in the next section.

The second master tool of persuasion: *questions*

Questions can:
☛ find out what is really going on in your prospect's head.
☛ find out what their real motivations are.
☛ find out their beliefs about life, people and you.
☛ test close.
☛ take pressure off.
☛ show you really care.
☛ build rapport.
☛ induce reciprocation.
☛ put people in a specific state.
☛ overcome objections.
☛ bring out objections.

The quality of your questions determines the quality of your life. Questions are the single most powerful tool you have to persuade people. When you ask a question, you take control and focus your prospect's mind. If you ask emotional questions, you cause a person to go into an emotional state.

It is vital for you as a Champion Salesperson to be able to put your prospects in the state of mind and mood you want, based upon your goals for influencing them at that moment in time. Telling people things does not persuade people half as much as getting them to tell you.

Remember the 80:20 rule of selling, which states simply: 80 per cent of the time you are with a prospect, the prospect should be talking. What's more, most of the 20 per cent of the time that you are talking should be spent asking questions. A smart customer will evaluate your value to her not on the answers you provide, but by the questions you ask.

There are six powerful sets of questions you can use to get the results you desire:

1 Resource questions

Resource questions put your prospect into a very positive mental state. These are questions like: What are you most happy about in your life right now? What are you most proud of? What are you excited about? What has been your greatest success so far? What has been your greatest contribution to your company's or your people's success?

Once you have made them feel good about themselves, talk about your service.

2 Hurt questions

Hurt questions stir up the prospect's pain and dissatisfaction. They are especially valuable when the prospect doesn't have a strong conscious want for your product. These are questions like: What do you think your current supplier may not be providing you with right now? What do you think your people want that they may not be getting right now? What is the biggest obstacle to your performance right now? By staying with your current supplier who has served you for the past five years, don't you think you may be missing out on some new thinking? Does it worry you that your competition seems to be growing faster than you are?

Obviously, you need to handle hurt questions with care. The challenge is to stir up the hurt but not to flood the prospect with anxiety. The moment you have stirred the hurt, you need to gently remind the client that your service can help. One of the most powerful ways to do this is to share a case study with them where you have helped a customer in a similar situation.

If you were to ask me what my most powerful persuasion tool is, I would tell you: my ability to stir up the hurt and then draw on my experience to share a success story where I helped a client in a very similar situation to the one I am with at the moment. I consistently position myself as someone who has been where the client is afraid to go. I am their corporate radar system – I identify, anticipate and pre-empt problems before they happen.

3 Feedback questions

Feedback questions ensure that you and your prospect are humming on the same frequency. They are very simple questions that consistently probe the prospect's level of understanding and rapport with you. Feedback questions also allow you to keep track of the client's opinion about what you are saying.

Feedback questions can be as simple as: So what do you think? Am I making sense? Would you agree? Is this clear? How does that sound to you? Are you okay with that?

Feedback questions not only give you feedback; they also keep the client involved. Like all of us, our prospects' minds can wander while we are presenting. Feedback questions consistently bring their minds back into focus. What's more, by asking feedback questions, you are constantly complimenting the client by reminding them that you value their point of view. Feedback questions are important not just in a formal selling situation, but in any situation where you genuinely want to build a relationship based on open two-way communication with another person.

4 Belief and value questions

Belief and value questions empower you to uncover what motivates the client or prospect to act the way they do. They are your X-rays into your prospect's mind. As a rule, I always ask belief and value questions before I get into the hard business issues. I do this for one very simple reason: If you don't know what the prospect's values and beliefs are, you don't know why they do what they do; you don't have a guide to their decision-making process; you cannot anticipate their desires – it's like flying blind.

Examples of belief and value questions are: What's most important to you when it comes to …? What do you look for the most in the people you choose to do business with? What has to happen for you to feel satisfied in …? Who do you admire the most? Why? What are the things you want to avoid the most in business? What are the values of your company? What kind of culture are you building here? What makes your top performers successful?

5 Test close questions

Test close questions test the barometer of desire within the prospect. They are the kind of questions you ask when you think you are near to making the sale, but when it is still too early to ask for the sale. They are very powerful questions because they tell you whether you are drawing nearer or drifting away from the final close. They also help the customer commit to you by expressing their favourable intent.

Examples of test close questions are: In your opinion, is this the kind of service that you believe could be valuable to your company? If budget were not an issue, would you invest in this product? In your opinion, if you were to go ahead with this, would you want it in blue or green? If you were able to persuade your colleagues about the merits of this programme, would you go for the full-day or two-day programme?

The main difference between test close questions and closing questions are that test close questions allow the prospects to voice their opinion without finally committing to your product or service. They are making a 'pre-commitment' without pressure.

Test close questions form your guidance system. Make sure you are armed with key test close questions before you visit prospects. These questions allow you to change course in mid-air if you have to. Remember that the person with the most flexibility always wins.

6 Close questions

Close questions ask for the sale. The major reason why many people never achieve their desires is that they are afraid to ask for them. We are sometimes more afraid of the little word 'no' than we are of hell itself. In fact, for many of us, rejection is hell.

My personal code of conduct commands me to always ask for what I desire. Even if I know that there is a 99 per cent chance of rejection, like asking for a free upgrade on SAA, I will still ask for what I want. It's my way of conditioning myself and toughening myself against rejection at the same time. What's more, every time I hear the word 'No!', I know I'm one step closer to hearing the magic sound: 'Yes!!'

Recently I was on a business trip to Port Elizabeth with a friend of mine named Duncan Phillips. We finished our business by lunchtime and we retired to a beachfront bar called Barney's for lunch. We each had a beer and a steak roll for lunch. The bill came to R70. I then asked Duncan what he thought the waitress would do if I said to her when she bought the bill, 'Write your own tip.'

Duncan said he thought I would be in deep shit. He said she would probably take me for a couple of hundred rand. 'On the contrary,' I replied, 'I think she'll be confused.' Sure enough, when Tracy, the waitress, came with the bill and handed me a pen, I gave it back to her and told her to write her own tip. She just looked at me, dumbfounded. Her eyes seemed to say, 'Why are you doing this to me?' After a couple seconds, I asked her how much of a tip she wanted. Do you know what her response was? Yeah, you guessed it. She said, 'I usually get ten per cent.' And that's what we gave her: a R7 tip.

Life will give you whatever you ask of it. But you have to ask. And you have to keep asking until you get what you want. The future belongs to the bold, the thick-skinned and the persistent. God's delays are not God's denials. I believe that we are put through one test after another until the Big Salesperson in the sky decides it's time for reward. And then we are showered with success as long as we keep passing our tests.

So when your intuition and your test close questions tell you it's time to ask for the order, do not hesitate. Ask, ask, ask. But ask in such a way that the prospect is encouraged to say yes. In my business as a coach and personal developer, here are some of my close questions: Okay, so I should book you for 22 October? How many workbooks should I bring? Would you like me to do the Maximum Influence programme or the Power to Persuade programme with your people? Will we be doing my half-day or full-day programme? Will you be giving your people *Lost and Found* or *Fire & Water* as a conference gift?

Before you move on to the next magical master tool of persuasion, review the preceding categories of questions. Formulate your own questions according to each category and then practise applying them as soon as possible.

Start right now. A Champion Salesperson never procrastinates. You have no time to waste time. After all, the biggest deal of your life may bump into you in the following hour. Are you ready to exploit it or not? Make sure you prepare yourself. He who hesitates is not only lost, but miles from the next opportunity.

The third master tool of persuasion:
your own personal congruency

You are congruent when what you say verbally and non-verbally match. That's when people believe you, because your words, your voice and your actions all reinforce each other. You are incongruent when what you are saying and what you are feeling are not unified, even when it is just a perception in other people's minds. Saying one thing and feeling another is the quickest way to lose a sale. Remember that people buy primarily for emotional reasons. To make an emotional decision they need to feel certain that what you are saying is true. If you aren't congruent, you will send out an aura of indecision and weakness. Your personal congruency is your ability to project absolute certainty in voice, word and body that what you are saying is accurate.

Think about a time when incongruency has cost you sales in the past. Think about how your lack of certainty cost you the sale.

How could you create more certainty about the value of your product so that incongruency doesn't ever cost you again in the future?

You will be congruent when:

☛ you act in accordance with your values.
☛ you are certain about what you are saying.
☛ you are truthful.
☛ you care deeply about the well-being of the person you're selling to.
☛ you believe that you're contributing much more value than you are taking back in any transaction.
☛ you are excited about what you are doing.

Beware of the law of familiarity and the AAK

At the age of a few months old, we all receive vaccination against smallpox. That vaccination lasts us our entire lives. However, vaccination against taking things for granted has to happen every day. The law of familiarity states that anytime you are around something long enough, you will begin to take it for granted and you will begin to lose your enthusiasm for it. That's why we tend to take our loved ones for granted. That's why we begin to take our most important clients for granted.

Until we receive an AAK: an **A**ttitude **A**djustment **K**lap – that's when what we've taken for granted gets taken away. Then, all of a sudden, we become overcome with regret and remorse. Has it ever happened to you? Well, it's happened to me big time. That's why my greatest strength today is my congruency.

When I was locked in the nightmare world of depression, I made a deal with my Higher Power. I said to Him, 'God, if you give me back my joy and lust for life, I'll never take anything for granted again and I'll spend the rest of my life helping others to do the same.' That's why this book is just another instalment on my debt with the Divine. From this moment on, consistently go for the magic in the mundane. Look for the extraordinary in the ordinary. Celebrate those who have already given you their support and loyalty. And be aware of wonder.

The fourth master tool of influence: *anchoring*

Anchoring is what selling is all about. An anchor simply means that a person has learnt to associate a certain feeling or meaning with something specific. The South African flag is a visual anchor: we have learned to associate definite feelings with those colours and shapes. 'Everything keeps going right' is an example of a sound anchor. Every time we hear that phrase, we think of Toyota.

There are also smell and feel anchors. Have you noticed how often you smell something and you immediately associate it with an event that you've experienced?

When your name is mentioned or when people see you, what kind of associations or feelings do they attach to you? Unless people anchor their most desirable feelings or meanings to you, your product or your service, you can never be a Master Persuader. The customers of Master Persuaders also associate being able to avoid painful experiences by owning their product or using their service.

How do anchors happen? An anchor is created when some unique stimulus occurs when a person is at the peak of an intense state of emotion. For example, let's say you met someone really special at a party and you were really attracted to him or her. You asked that person to dance, and as you danced cheek-to-cheek you listened to the song that was playing. At that moment, you may have linked the song to your feelings of joy and excitement. Or let's say you were in a crisis and someone who works with you came into your office, smiled and helped you with your problem. Anytime you saw that person smiling in the future, you may have anchored him or her to your feelings of gratitude and relief.

Pavlov and his dogs: do you make your customers salivate?

For an anchor to become powerful, the same stimulus must consistently occur when we are in an intense state, so that the two become linked in our nervous systems.

Most of us have heard of Pavlov and the work he did with dogs, where food was used as a trigger to put the dogs in a certain state of satisfaction. Simultaneously during those moments, bells were rung until the dog began to associate ringing bells with food. Initially, only the food made the dog salivate, but later just a ringing bell would create the saliva. So, just like the dogs when they heard the bell, do your customers salivate when they think of you? Do they associate massive pleasure with dealing with you? How can you begin to build that association right now?

Almost all advertising is simple anchoring devices. Watch commercials from now on and ask yourself: What kind of feelings is the advertiser attempting to get me to associate with their product or service? People don't buy products; they buy the states that the advertiser has associated with their product. Toyota sells the state of reliability; BMW sells the state of driving pleasure and performance; Mercedes sells the anchor of prestige.

The key is to discover what states or feelings your customers want and then get them to associate those feelings with you, your product or your service. I, for example, get my customers to associate me with a state of excitement and optimism. Everything I do when it comes to selling, I do with the intention of strengthening the bond between me and the feelings of excitement I create. That's what this book is: another demonstration of excitement in action.

During my programmes, I let people repeatedly stand up, pump their arms up and down and shout the word 'Yes!!' as loud as they can. I've even created a range of 'Yes!!' T-shirts. Now, when I meet people who have attended my programme, the first thing they do is shout the word 'Yes!!'.

Traditional selling theory teaches 'sell the benefits, not the features, of your product'. And that's right. But it's also only the first step in the selling process. The real objective is to sell your customer or prospect the desired state they want to be in.

What can you do to anchor the things your customers want most with you or your product? How can you get others to associate you with their desired states? How can you make them salivate when they hear your name?

The fifth master tool of persuasion: *pattern interrupts*

What people do is based on the state they are in at any moment in time. We all have had the experience of trying to speak or sell to someone when they are not in a state to listen or when they have anchored negative feelings to us or our products. In order to get them to listen to us or to buy from us, we first have to interrupt their negative thought patterns. We have to open their minds so that they will at least give us a chance to persuade them. We have to replace their negative associations with positive ones.

I am often faced with the challenge of interrupting someone's negative perception of me or my service. I am told that 'motivational speakers' and 'salesmen' are merely conmen and charlatans. I interrupt my prospect's negative thought pattern by saying to him or her, 'Maybe you're right. But have you ever saved a teenager's life, or helped someone who thought they had no wings to soar into the sky? Have you given hope to a no-hoper and have you healed a broken soul?' This response immediately breaks their thought pattern and gets them to think of me in a new light. I then share with them how I have managed those feats before I sell them my products or service. I get people into a positive mental and emotional state before I start talking about my products or services.

All of us have been in a situation where we were making a point to someone when they asked us a question that distracted us. We, therefore, forgot what we were saying in the first place. This is known as 'pattern interrupts'. We can use this technique to get people out of a negative state. The next time you are with someone who seems stuck in a negative state, ask them an unexpected question that breaks their pattern. They will have a hard time getting back to their objections and they may even forget it completely, allowing you to close the sale. Master Persuaders are master pattern interrupters.

Think about how you can interrupt other people's negative thought patterns in a respectful yet playful way. Practise doing it as soon as possible.

The sixth master tool of persuasion: *framing skills*

Everything we do is based on how we are feeling at that particular moment, and our feelings are based on what we are focusing on at that moment. Whatever you think about at any moment dictates your mood. If you are in a bad mood right now, it's because you are concentrating on what puts you in a bad mood. Conversely, if you are feeling happy right now, it's because you are thinking about something that makes you happy.

To change people's behaviour, we have to change the way they feel. To change the way they feel, we have to change what they are focusing on. At any moment in time, we can only focus on one thing at a time. The Master Persuader helps to direct what a prospect focuses on; he directs how they feel and what they'll do in a given situation. He achieves this by applying his framing skills.

The three framing skills that Master Persuaders use are:

1 The 'as if' frame: changing the focus of the customer
Often a person will tell you that they can't do something or that something is impossible. If you try and tell them that it is possible, they resist you because you are fighting their belief systems. All that will result from your words is conflict and friction. Instead, the challenge is to get your prospect or customer to focus on possibilities.

Suppose a person says to you, 'I can't buy now. There is no possible way.' It will not help you to contradict them and tell them that they can buy now. Instead, you could respond, 'I know you're not going to buy. But let me ask you a question: If for some reason, you did decide to buy, what would it be that changed your mind?'

By asking an 'as if' question, you get the other person to stop focusing on why something can't be done and start focusing on why it could. Often, this kind of question not only provides a solution to the problem, but it also puts the prospect in a new state that encourages them to buy. The 'as if' question eliminates the obstacle from the discussion and focuses on possibility.

One of the things that continues to amuse me in my seminars is when I ask someone a question that they cannot answer. The person just says to me, 'I don't know.' Now, if I were to tell them that they did know the answer, they would just get annoyed. Instead, I say to them, 'I know you don't know the answer. But if you did know, what do you think it might be?' Often they then give me an answer, because I have taken the focus away from giving me the 'right' answer to an answer that is merely 'possible'. As soon as you change someone's focus, you change how they feel and what they do.

Other 'as if' questions are:
☛ If we did do that, what might happen?
☛ Let's just say we did work it out, just suppose ... .
☛ If we could do something with the price, would you buy?

2 Preframing: controlling the focus of the customer in advance

This is the name I developed for what I've seen Master Persuaders do time and time again. They prevent objections by handling them in advance. They kill the monster while it's tiny. Before a customer has an opportunity to focus on what may be wrong with a particular proposition, the Master Salesperson directs their focus ahead of the objection. In other words, they pre-empt the problem – they 'preframe' the customer.

Let's say I am a real estate salesperson and I am going to show you a home that's great for your price range and situated in the kind of environment you want for your family, but it's 80 kilometres outside the city where you work. I am not going to wait until we get to the home, by which time you have begun to focus on how much time it takes you to travel back and forth from work each day.

Instead, I would direct your focus by framing you on what living there would mean. I would say something like, 'John, I can't wait to show you this home. It's everything you've ever dreamed of. It's on an acre of land; it's got a country environment for your kids; it's safe; it's right by a river and best of all, it's 80 kilometres outside the traffic, grime and crime of the city. It's close enough to get into the city and get your work done and it still allows you to have the home you've always wanted.'

In essence what I've done is framed you in advance about what to focus on. I've framed you to focus on the meaning of this home being 80 kilometres outside the city as a point of pleasure not pain.

A preframe I use with busy people who I want to attend my seminars is: 'A lot of people say to me that they don't have the time to attend seminars. When I hear that, I can't even believe it. Can you imagine someone saying they don't have enough time to learn the skills that could increase their sales by up to 200 per cent? Isn't that stupid?' Most times, after hearing me tell them that, people sign up for the course.

Another way I preframe people to attend my programmes is by describing the kind of people who do attend my programmes as follows: 'You know,' I say, 'a lot of people don't care about their self-image or maximizing their true potential or massively contributing to the people around them. They just want to survive, make the sale and carry on the way they always have. My programme is designed for people who are really committed to absolutely living their life at the highest level, to being the best they can possibly be for themselves, for their family, for their friends. They are people who are committed to being outstanding. People who don't share this drive to be a champion don't attend my seminars; it's just too much trouble.'

By telling my prospects about the kind of people who attend my programmes, I get them to automatically include themselves in the class of people who want to be champions – through attending my programme.

The ABC of selling

Have you attended my Sales Mastery programme? Are you one of the few who do versus the many who talk? Would you like to take yourself to the next level? How would you feel if I could improve your sales effectiveness by 100 per cent in just one day?

Take action now. Send me your name, position, the name of your company and your postal address to: Mike Lipkin Seminars, PO Box 41882, Craighall, 2024, South Africa. Or fax me on (011) 728-6907.

Why do you think I have just tried to get you take action? Obviously I want to have the privilege of sharing my knowledge with you. But what I really wanted to demonstrate here was the ABC of selling: **Always Be Clos-**

ing. At every point in the sale or discussion, seize the opportunity to get your prospect or customer to take action.

Are you a great personal marketer?

Another way of preframing your customer is through outstanding personal marketing. By personal marketing, I mean 'preframing' your prospect to have certain expectations of you in advance of meeting you. This can be achieved through word of mouth advertising where your existing clients talk highly of you to prospects, or it can be done through mailings that you've sent to the prospect in advance of meeting them. What do you think advertising is? It is simply a way of preframing prospects to view a product or service in a certain way.

I have found that the most powerful way I have of 'preframing' customers is simply to send them a package containing testimonials of delighted clients of mine. I then follow up with a phone call and a meeting. Remember that Master Persuaders make the sale before they even get in front of the client. If you have not preframed the prospect to buy beforehand, you have not done enough groundwork on your personal image.

Preframing is the essence of proactivity in selling. It is controlling events before they happen. It is leadership in action. It is the consistent anticipation of what happens next. If you are a 'preframer', you are someone with a highly developed personal radar system. You tend to sense opportunities before most other people do.

One of the most powerful skills that preframers have is their ability to rapidly establish rapport. They understand that rapport is the most important ingredient in highly successful relationships, so they move upfront to achieve it. So, as a self-acknowledged preframer, I always focus on the human issues before I focus on the business issues. I make sure my prospect understands three things about me immediately:

☛ I am totally committed to him or her. I genuinely want them to be successful.

☛ I am passionate about what I do and I automatically assume they are also passionate about their work.

☛ I am in it for the long term. The first assignment I get from my client is merely that: the first instalment on a mutually rewarding, enduring relationship.

Are you a preframer? How developed is your personal radar system? Do you take the bull by the horns or does the bull take you?

3 Reframing: redirecting the customer's focus

No matter how skilled you are as a preframer, there will always be the need to handle objections that you haven't anticipated in advance. Reframing means being able to redirect the customer's focus so that you change the way they look at the situation.

Remember, people are always asking themselves two primary questions:
☞ What does this mean to me?
☞ What should I do?

Let's go back to the real estate example. Suppose I am a real estate agent and you are my prospect. We drive out to the house we discussed. You like the house in a lot of ways, but you begin to focus on the fact that it's 80 kilometres outside the city where you work. You associate that distance with inconvenience and you say to me, 'Mike, it's a great house but it's 80 kilometres from town.'

My reframe to you might be, 'Well, Jane, is it how far you are from the city or how long it takes for you to get there?' (Notice that the question here is changing the focus: The frame is being changed from distance to time.)

You say, 'Well, how long it takes is probably more important.'

I then respond to you as follows: 'Well then, let me ask you this question: How much longer do you think it will take you to get into town versus the other place you are considering?'

You say, 'Oh, about 20 minutes.'

I say, 'Well, let me ask you a question. I might be wrong, but wouldn't it be worth an additional 20 minutes more a day in order to live where you really want to live? And wouldn't it also be worth the entirely reasonable price to have your family live in the environment that they've always dreamed of? Or would you rather live 20 minutes closer to the city in a place that doesn't meet your true needs and compromises your family's well-being?'

This example demonstrates the application and power of reframing. I changed the focus of being 80 kilometres from the city from being negative to positive. Now when Jane compares the emotional reasons for buying the house I want to sell her, her reasons to buy would be much stronger than her reasons for not buying. I redirected her focus.

Ask yourself how you will be able to redirect your customer's focus from negative consequences to positive ones. What are their most common objections and how could you turn them around through the power of reframing?

The seventh master tool of persuasion:
time and energy mastery

Remember this golden rule: *The more time you spend with your prospects and customers face to face, the more fun you will have, the more you will sell and the more you will earn.*

People often ask me for my ultimate secret of success. They expect me to give them the 'open sesame' magical secret. Well, here's my Abracadabra: *The more opportunities you get to sell, the more you will sell.* Life is a numbers game. Even with all my sales, I still hear the word 'No!' more than the word 'Yes!'. But I've narrowed the odds. What's more, because I've learned to organize my time in such a way that I maximize my 'face time' with customers, I am getting a whole lot more chances to sell. Hence, my sales productivity has gone through the roof.

I could write a book on time management. There are, in fact, many books on the subject. I don't believe, however, that we can reduce time management to an absolute science, especially in selling. There are just too many unexpected things that happen every day.

What we can do, though, is to design a plan for our time that will enable us to spend most of our time with customers and prospects. No matter how many skills you have or how effective a persuader you are, your bottom line is impacted primarily by where you spend most of your face-to-face time. How do you spend your time? Is it in planning or is it face to face with customers?

Obviously you need a plan, but the planning should happen during non-sales times, like before 09:00, after 17:00 and over weekends. All Master Persuaders have learned to master their selling time. They have mastered themselves to live in their clients' offices or sites, not their own.

Become a sales athlete!

The most powerful force in the universe is a salesperson who works eight hours a day face to face with customers; not just a salesperson who keeps himself busy. Anyone can be busy. We've all heard of Parkinson's law: 'Our work will expand to the amount of time we give it.' There are so many salespeople I meet who will do anything to actually minimize their time in front of the customer. Why? Because it takes mental toughness, resilience and extreme energy to keep on getting in front of a customer and delivering a virtuoso sales performance. You cannot afford to give in to your physical fatigue or mental tiredness. Just like an Olympic athlete, you have to train yourself to keep on going. Make a commitment to yourself to take yourself to the next level. When you just cannot see another customer or make another call, just make it. Love those rejections. Savour the 'No'. Stretch those selling muscles. Very soon, you will condition yourself to do more, be more, sell more.

You have to be physically fit to sustain the pace of a Master Persuader. Have you ever noticed how sexy we find people who are in great shape? Have you ever been close to a professional athlete and sensed their vitality? I've discovered that when I am not physically tuned up, my performance suffers greatly. I make sure that I work out at least five times a week. What's your level of physical fitness? Have you got the horsepower to go the extra mile every day? Have you got the stamina to outlast your competition? Do you radiate health and vitality? If not, begin a physical development programme today! If you smoke, stop immediately. You cannot be a smoker and be healthy. What's more, the biggest sin you can commit as a salesperson is to smoke in front of your prospect or customer. By smoking, you broadcast the fact that you lack personal pride, discipline and self-control.

Networking: the most underdeveloped client development tool in South Africa

Master Persuaders make sure they get in the way of opportunity. They sell by wandering around. They have learned how to network. They attend the right functions. They are active in developing their respective markets and industries. They don't give of their time because they are good Samaritans. They give of their time because they know it's an investment that will pay out over time. I make sure that at least 15 per cent of my talks and seminars are sessions I do not deliver for profit. They are my one-man contribution to the RDP or GEAR. And you know what? Every time I give a free talk, I get work from it, because somewhere in the audience there is a prospect who was impressed by what I said.

Make very sure that you network within your client companies. Most of my clients are the top 200 companies in South Africa: South African Breweries, Standard Bank, ABSA, Investec, Pick 'n Pay, Engen, Caltex, Shell, Nissan, Toyota, Mercedes Benz, and so on. Whenever I go to these companies for a meeting, I wander around the building and visit other prospects within the company. Remember, your mission and mine is to stay 'top of mind' with the clients. That means to stay visible so that when an opportunity arises, they immediately think of you. Does this make sense to you? I know it does. Start practising it now!

A foundation for success

Session Four

The six secrets of creating inner pressure to buy

Purpose and outcome of this session

Would you like to know how to make people make a decision you want them to make because they believe that they are making it for their own reasons? That's exactly what I'm going to share with you in this session. I am going to show you how to use the six principles of creating inner pressure to buy, to persuade your prospects to buy from you. Best of all, I am going to show you how to do this without appearing to exert any undue external pressure.

As a result of completing this session, you'll be able to:

- ☛ identify the most powerful psychological influences that affect human decision-making and use them elegantly and with integrity to create a powerful, almost compulsive, need to buy in the mind of the prospect.
- ☛ plan and apply each of these principles to your own particular selling situation.

The six secrets of creating inner pressure to buy

How do we really make decisions? Most of us would be surprised at the outside influences that have a subconscious impact on what we do. Many of these influences have no basis in logic whatsoever. Instead, they are the result of deep emotional programming that comes from our past, our family, our culture, our expectations and our beliefs. Some of these influences empower us and some of them disempower us. The challenge is to understand them so that we can use them to persuade others as well as ourselves.

I often say to audiences at my seminars that one of the reasons I am so motivated is that I attend all my own talks. Inevitably, that comment gets a laugh. But I'm serious when I say it. I am continually talking to myself and evaluating why I'm doing what I'm doing. If I find myself in the grip of fear or anxiety, I ask myself why I'm feeling that way. I isolate the real reason why I'm in a certain state and then I take appropriate action to motivate myself. I've become my own best coach not my own worst enemy. And you know what I've discovered: *99 per cent of the time* the influences which drive me are the result of the meaning I attach to what's happening around me – not the events themselves.

Nothing in life has any meaning except the meaning you give it. The next time you are feeling any kind of negative emotion that is stopping you from being a Master Persuader, ask yourself whether you are applying the right meaning to the situation or whether, by changing your interpretation of events, you can change your mood and your motivation. The reasons which you think are pulling you down are almost never the real reasons: the real reasons are how you interpret the outside events.

Let's look at the six secrets of creating inner pressure to buy or, described in a different way, the six principles of unconscious persuasion. I guarantee you that if you can master these six principles, your effectiveness as a persuader will soar.

1 The 'because' frame

There are certain words that trigger us to go on automatic pilot: We stop evaluating what we should do and we just comply. One of these words is 'because'. The need for reasons to justify behaviour is so strong within human beings that we have learned to anchor the word 'because' to thinking that someone has justified reasons for doing something. When you were a kid and your parents refused you permission to do something you wanted to do, what did you do? Did you accept 'no' for an answer? I don't think so. You asked, 'Why not?' How many times did your parents respond, 'Just because' or 'Because I said so!' or 'Because that's the way it is!'?

Social researchers have found that our programming to accept the word 'because' as justification for doing something is so strong that even if what is said after the word 'because' doesn't make sense, over 90 per cent of people will still comply as if there were a legitimate reason to do so. The word 'because' triggers compliance.

This tool is extremely useful because we automatically say no to things. It's easier to say no than to say yes, because yes implies commitment. Remember that the next time you hear the word 'no'.

How many times have you entered a store and the store assistant has asked you, 'Can I help you?' What's your normal immediate response, unless you have a specific want you need satisfied? How about, 'No, thank you, I'm just looking'? If someone gives you an automatic rejection like in the store example, you can just say, 'Okay, that's fine. I just need to stay here with you because I need to support you in answering questions' or 'I need to stay with you because my boss told me to.'

Many times all people need is a 'because' frame. They need to feel that you have a justifiable reason for doing something. The actual reason may be less important than the fact that you have offered them a 'because'. Think about how many times you have acted because of the way someone gave you a reason rather than the reason itself. The secret of persuasion lies in the way something is told to you rather than what is being told to you. I'm not saying you can talk absolute nonsense and get away with it. What I am saying is that you should always provide people with a 'because'; a feasible reason why they should do something. Start practising the 'because' frame today.

2 The law of contrast

Whatever people decide to do is based on how they evaluate things. We are always comparing things and people to each other and to ourselves.

The law of contrast is a way to immediately change someone's evaluations of how difficult, how easy, how expensive or how cheap something is. In order to make a decision, we have to compare things. What we compare them to plays a huge role in determining whether we believe something is worthwhile or not, worth doing or not, expensive or not. Someone who lives in a R2 million house may not think R200 000 to put in a heated swimming pool is expensive. But someone who lives in a R200 000 home may think it's exorbitant.

The law of contrast states that anytime you compare two things that are different side by side, they will appear more different than they actually are. This law can be used to condition your prospect's expectations. Look at how effective the 'before and after' commercials for companies like Weight Watchers are. When we view the before and after pictures side by side, we are struck by the extent of the weight loss. Another example is the 'info-mercials' for products that we see on television. The voice-over sounds something like this, 'How much would you expect to pay for a machine that could change your life and make you slim and strong and sexy and successful and attractive and irresistible? Would R5 000 be too much to pay for a machine that could change your life? Well, for this week only you can acquire this extraordinary machine for just R999! And that's not all … but wait, there's more … ' You may be smiling cynically to yourself as you read these words, but they work and they work well. That's why you will continue to see and hear them day after day.

In property negotiations, the buyer will often put in a very low bid so that the seller is conditioned to expect a lower price. When the buyer then puts in a higher bid but still lower than what the seller originally wanted, the seller may accept the price because it doesn't seem so low compared to the original price.

I often try and persuade companies who hire me to speak or train their people to buy books or tapes in addition to the workshop. I will offer them a book and a tape package at, say, R90. But I will tell them that they sell separately for R60 each. The prospect then does their calculations, works out that I am offering them a 25 per cent discount and is more motivated to buy. Every 'Sale' ad that you see in the newspapers uses this principle. They compare the price you would normally pay to the price they are offering you on 'Sale'. You work out the savings and decide to buy or not.

Another way I use the law of contrast to justify my fees (which are not cheap) is to compare the cost per delegate to my seminar versus the value the company will get from the delegate once they have been through my seminar. If the cost per delegate is R500 and the delegate is in the business of selling cars, I say to the decision-maker, 'You make R2 000 on every car sold. That means if I can get your salesperson to sell just one more car this month, you will get a 300 per cent return on your investment in the next 30 days.' Needless to say, my prospect sends the delegate. So right now, ask yourself how you can use the law of contrast to motivate others to make the decision you want them to make.

The law of contrast is also a powerful gratitude booster.

So far, we have discussed the law of contrast as a tool to get others to make the decisions you want them to make. But it can also be used as a powerful way to motivate yourself. People often ask me how I manage to be so excited almost all the time. I tell them that I keep comparing my current situation to the situation I was in six years ago when I was so depressed I needed shock therapy to come right. Even today, I still cannot believe how lucky I am.

A few months ago, I spoke to 1 500 people at IBM South Africa. The talk went extremely well. As I stood in front of all these wildly cheering people, I almost cried with gratitude as I thought of how far I had come since the dark days of 1991. What's more, I often compare myself to the thousands of South Africans I see every day who have almost nothing and yet their spirit is full. Compared to them, I say to myself, I have everything. I have no right to be depressed – ever! Remember the old saying: 'I had the blues because I had no shoes – until on the street, I met a man who had no feet.'

3 The law of reciprocation

One of the most powerful tools of unconscious persuasion we can use is the law of reciprocation. We are conditioned to believe that if someone gives something to you, you need to give something back, or if someone does us a favour, we need to return it. How many times have you heard people say to someone else who has helped them, 'I owe you one'? How many times have you felt the need to 'return the favour'? How many times have you told someone you like them after they have told you they liked you? If someone invites you to dinner, don't you feel the need to reciprocate? How many times have you said to someone who has done something for you, 'Much obliged'? In your own mind you are obliged to the other person to return the favour. People will do more for others out of the pressure of obligation than almost any other source.

When someone does something for us, we begin to experience an unconscious, and sometimes conscious, pressure to reciprocate. If we don't reciprocate, we begin to experience pressure build-up or even discomfort. The need to reciprocate is therefore more than just a desire to return a favour. It is a programmed pattern installed in most of us. Think about the consequences for you if you don't give back when someone gives to you. How are you perceived by others? Aren't you perceived as a taker, a leech, someone who doesn't care or who is stingy? On the other hand, if you give to others far more than they ever give to you, you are perceived as generous, trustworthy, a friend, loyal and supportive.

Anytime you can do a favour for a prospect, do so. You've just made a deposit into the emotional bank account. You've just invested in the most valuable asset you can ever have: relationships. People often ask me why they should keep giving when they haven't yet received a reciprocation from the other person. I respond by telling them to keep giving if they want the prospect's business intensely enough. There will come a time when the prospect feels compelled to give back. Remember that Master Persuaders have patience and tenacity in the pursuit of their dreams.

Begin practising the law of reciprocation right now. Identify your key prospects and plan how you can begin depositing in the emotional bank account. Think of at least five ways in which you can use the law of reciprocation to induce deep gratitude in your prospects. Think about how you can generate in your prospects a desire, a need to pay you back in a way that supports them and supports you with integrity.

4 The power of double binds

The fourth secret of creating inner pressure to buy is the power of double binds. A double bind is when you give someone the illusion of choice when, in reality, whatever solution they take, they're still doing what you would like them to do. You therefore do not give them the opportunity to say 'no'. Obviously, this tool can only be used when you are convinced that the prospect needs your product and that fear is the only thing that is stopping them.

The key element that makes a double bind work is the word 'or'. The word 'or' is like 'because': it immediately puts people on automatic pilot because 'or' gives them the illusion of choice. They therefore evaluate the choice you are offering them less critically, especially in the moment when you want them to make a decision. However, it is important that you continue talking with a double bind after you have given the prospect the illusion of choice. And you must ask a question shortly afterwards.

These are two examples of double binds that I use:

☛ When I try to make an appointment with a prospect: 'Would you like to make an appointment right now *or* would you just like to jot down a time for us to get together? *Because* I'm sure the thing that is most important to you is to create the results that you really want for your company. Isn't that true?'

☛ When I try to get the prospect to hire me to train their people: 'Would you like me to deliver a workshop with your people *or* would you like me to do a morning motivational session with them? *Because* I know you want highly motivated Master Persuaders to sell your services. Am I right?'

Double binds are extremely effective ways to close the sale or even test close the sale. Right now, design two double binds that will help you to motivate your prospects to make the kind of decisions you want them to make. Experiment with them. Have some fun! *Moenie bang wees nie!*

5 The law of social proof

The fifth secret of creating inner pressure to buy is the law of social proof. This law simply states that if enough people are doing something or if the *right* people are doing something, we begin to perceive it as appropriate behaviour for ourselves. This is true even in situations that don't always make sense, like when people get on to drugs because they see enough of their peers doing it; or when people walk on hot coals because they see other people doing it without harm. Psychologists have shown over and over again that when people are uncertain about what to do, they look to others to see what to do. This is known as the principle of adaptation. We learn by watching others.

The law of social proof is probably the most widely used advertising principle of all. Think about the OMO ads that feature testimonials from hundreds of ordinary women testifying to the power of OMO. Or think about all the advertising that features well-known and respected people. Think about the Nike or Reebok advertising that features well-known sports people. Or think about how many times you've seen the words 'Thousands of South Africans can't be wrong' or 'South Africa's best-selling car' or 'South Africa's favourite food' or 'The name trusted by thousands of South Africans'.

Your challenge is how to use the law of social proof to get people to buy into you. Let me share my experience with you: In 1993, when I decided to become an entrepreneur in charge of my own destiny, I knew I needed to do something that would get me the social proof to build credibility with the South African business community. For five months, I focused on this single challenge because I knew the right social proof would be my Abracadabra to success.

The answer came to me one morning at about 2 a.m. I knew because I looked at the clock next to my bed as I jumped up in excitement. I decided to write a book on the key mind-set changes South Africans needed to make in order to be successful in the future. However, on my own, the book would never sell because no one knew or even cared who I was. My breakthrough idea was to write the book with Reg Lascaris, one of South Africa's best-known and respected advertising executives. By writing the book with Reg Lascaris, I would gain instant credibility, because Reg's social proof would transfer on to me by association. As it so happens, my timing was perfect, because Reg wanted to write another book, having already co-authored two national best-sellers. He agreed to do the book with me and the end result was *Revelling in the Wild: Business Lessons out of Africa*. This book has sold over 20 000 copies and continues to sell even now.

I then followed up with *Lost and Found: My Journey to Hell and Back*, which also sold over 20 000 copies. Two years later, I co-authored another book with Reg called *Fire & Water: The Power of Passion, the Force of Flow*, which has also sold almost 20 000 copies. I am certain this book will achieve the same success.

Why am I telling you this? Because the fact that over 60 000 intelligent South Africans have read my words gives me powerful social proof. That's probably why you bought this book in the first place.

You don't have to write books to get social proof. Referrals are often all the social proof you need. When I am trying to convert a prospect to my services, I show him a selection of the most persuasive testimonials I have received from delighted clients. Don't cold-call anymore. Warm up your prospect in advance through referrals, testimonials and gifts that initiate the law of reciprocation.

Other ways to win social proof include getting publicity by speaking at key industry events; contributing to magazine and newspaper articles; getting people to talk about you to their associates by delivering magnificent service that amazes and delights them. Right now, think about what you need to do to get the law of social proof working for you.

6 The law of consistency

The sixth secret of creating inner pressure to buy is the law of consistency. Once we take a stand on something or commit to a certain point of view, we have a deeply felt need to remain consistent with that stand or point of view. Others perceive people who are consistent to be dependable, trustworthy and someone with whom they want to associate. People who are inconsistent are seen to be undependable, undesirable and best avoided.

In other words, people who are consistent are seen to have backbone; they are people who follow through; they are winners and achievers. That's why whenever we take a stand on something, we have inner pressure to remain consistent with our original point of view. This pressure can be so strong that it has the potential to limit our lives. That's why many people find it so hard to change or to admit that they made a mistake.

In selling, the law of consistency can be used to get people to take action. One of the easiest ways to get people to purchase something is to show them that not buying your product would be inconsistent with something that they already believe in, or with a value that they already hold. Conversely, you can show them that by buying your product they will act entirely consistent with their values or beliefs. If you sell life insurance and your prospect tells you that they don't want life insurance because they believe that it is a waste of money, you can show them (knowing that they care deeply about their family) that life insurance is consistent with the care that they have for their family. You could further show them that not to buy life insurance would be inconsistent with the commitment they have to their family. That will at least grab their attention. After you have their attention, you would have to keep referring to their family values throughout the presentation in order to guide them towards the sale. If you sell cars, and you know that your prospect has always bought the highest quality brand names and you wanted to sell them an expensive car, you might say, 'Don't you deserve the best? From what I have heard about you, it would seem out of place for you to be driving a car that is not the best of the best when everything else you have is the very best.'

When I am selling services, I constantly practise the law of consistency. I am known as a maverick. I help companies challenge their status quo and look for bold new ways of doing business. When I am in front of a prospect (on whom I have done my homework), I say, 'From what I have heard about your style, you are the kind of person who is continually looking for new ways to add value to your customers. That's exactly what my mission is. That's why we should be working together.'

If you can show a prospect how buying from you is consistent with their beliefs and values, and how not buying from you is inconsistent with a standard that they hold for themselves, they will almost have no choice but to buy.

Think about how you can use the law of consistency to increase your sales in a way that adds value to both yourself and your customers. Do you even know what your customers' or prospects' beliefs and values are? If you don't, you are missing out on one of the most potent selling techniques available to you.

Before you move on to the next section, review the six secrets to creating inner pressure to buy. Study them well. They will help you to unlock sales you never dreamed of. And even if you are not a professional salesperson, these secrets will help you convert people to your point of view elegantly and convincingly.

The most important sale you'll ever make!

Session One

Compelling reasons: how to unleash your power

The most important sale you'll ever make: 'you to you'

The most important sale you'll ever make is not to a particular customer that you are chasing; it is the sale called 'you to you'. *The ability to persuade yourself that what you have is much more valuable than any payment you would get back from the customer is the single most important element in your long-term sales success.*

In addition, you must have the ability to persuade yourself to make the calls that are necessary when you don't feel like it, to ask one more time after nine or ten noes, to consistently generate the levels of energy and enthusiasm that are necessary even when you're tired. What's more, you need to consciously guard against letting others see your fatigue or frustration. You need the beliefs that will sustain you during your down times. We have discussed these points briefly before and we will now explore them deeply. This level of persuasion, this level of unrelenting energy, this level of powerful belief is what sets the Sales Champions apart from those who are merely average.

There are three elements that can assist you in getting to Sales Championship level:

1   The development of compelling enough reasons to let you use your skills to the maximum.
2   Understanding, aligning and redirecting your customer's beliefs.
3   The ability to manage your mental, emotional and physical state when times are difficult.

What makes people succeed?

Have you ever seen two salespeople put side by side, where the one with less training and less resources outproduces the one who clearly has the greater natural ability and a better education?

The difference in sales performance is based on how much desire and intensity you have to use all of your power as a persuader. The objective of this session, therefore, is to help you to discover and to develop the compelling reasons that will drive you forward to use more of your ability and unleash your power to succeed. *Remember that success in life is 20 per cent how and 80 per cent why to succeed.*

Outcome and focus of this session

As a result of working through this session, you will:

☛ discover the three reasons why people fail to achieve what they want.
☛ identify a set of goals and, more importantly, a set of reasons that you can use to motivate yourself to peak performance even in difficult situations. You will begin to enjoy the excitement and benefits of having clearly defined goals.

There are three major reasons why most people fail to achieve what they want:

1 **They are unclear of what they want in the first place.** In order to make a dream come true, you first have to have a great dream. It continues to amaze me how few people have a clear vision of what they really want; for most people, it's just to stay alive between nine and five. What *I* really want, is to be acknowledged as South Africa's Number One Persuader and Communicator. This book is one of the ways that will help me to achieve that goal.

2 **People don't keep their commitments.** To make a commitment is the easiest thing in the world to do. But to not keep your commitments is also the easiest thing to do – both to yourself and to others. Nothing is more powerful when it comes to building relationships than keeping your commitments. And nothing is more destructive to relationships than not honouring your commitments. Unfortunately, salespeople are notorious for not honouring the commitments they have made.

3 **People don't create compelling enough reasons for following through when the going gets tough.** How many times have you started something with a great deal of enthusiasm and excitement, only to give it up a little later because you have lost interest or the desire to make it happen? That's how many people lead their lives. They start off well and then never finish what they started because they don't have compelling enough reasons to see it through.

Writing a book is like running a double mental Comrades Marathon. To give you some idea of what's involved, this book contains over 60 000 words, while the average letter is about 200 words. In order for me to have stayed the distance and finished this book on top of all my other work, I really had to have compelling reasons. They were:
☛ I want to keep taking myself to the next level. Growth is one of my most important values. I know that this book will help me to achieve that.

☛ I need to keep reinventing myself so I stay relevant to all the people I want to continue working with. My greatest fear is becoming yesterday's news.

☛ I get huge pleasure from publishing new books. When I see my books in print, I get intensely excited.

☛ I want to keep empowering people to take themselves where they've never been before. My purpose is 'to excite people into action'.

Written purpose and goals: the Abracadabra of making dreams come true

Have you ever processed the sun's rays through a magnifying glass until you reduced them to a tiny pinprick of light? Did you notice how the pinprick of light would burn its way through almost anything because of its focus and intensity? It's exactly the same with a written purpose and goals. Earlier on, we discussed the power of purpose. Have you thought about yours yet? By now, do you have an empowering personal mission that focuses your energy? Are you living on purpose or are you living by accident?

Take time right now to think about your purpose. Go back to the section where I discussed purpose with you. Do not continue reading until you have some sense of what your purpose truly is.

Welcome back. I know you now know your purpose! However, while your purpose remains timeless, you also need written goals that change every month or year. What's more, you need a written plan for attaining them. This is not difficult, but it does require the discipline to actually do it. Because if you fail to plan, you really plan to fail. In a Yale University study, they discovered that the five per cent of students in a class who had written goals and plans for their attainment made more money than the entire other 95 per cent of students combined.

What is a goal?

A goal is:

☛ a dream with a deadline.

☛ something that you are absolutely determined to have.

☛ something that fills you with a sense of pleasure and fulfilment when you achieve it.

☛ something that fills you with a deep sense of pain if you don't achieve it.

☛ a means to stretch and grow yourself.

- ☛ ambitious but within reach – it should be achievable, big and bold.
- ☛ the milestone by which you measure the achievement of your purpose.
- ☛ the measurable commitment you make to yourself.
- ☛ what gives focus and meaning to your life.
- ☛ always supported by compelling reasons for attaining it.
- ☛ clear and specific.
- ☛ something you can control, rather than things you cannot.
- ☛ the sail with which you control the wind.

My top four written one-year goals are:
- ☛ To stage ten major public events where I talk to at least 6 000 people.
- ☛ To achieve R5 million in turnover for my company.
- ☛ To be acknowledged by my prospects and customers as South Africa's number one persuader, motivator and sales empowerer.
- ☛ To publish a new best-selling book, successful sales course and audio programme.

A summary of my written plan for achieving those goals is:
- ☛ Develop quality relationships with the highest quality prospects and customers.
- ☛ Achieve top-of-mind awareness among discerning people by constantly featuring in the media.
- ☛ Grow by learning and bench-marking myself against the best in the world.
- ☛ Surround myself with strategic partners who are champions.
- ☛ Expand my circle of contacts to ensure that I am relevant to every South African.
- ☛ Provide myself with lots of recovery time so I don't burn out or go stale.

An easy, enjoyable, exciting six-step workshop to help you set your goals for the year ahead

Here is a really fun, six-step way to kick-start your goal-setting pro-gramme:

Step 1

For 15 minutes, write down anything and everything you want to do, be, have, create, give, share, discover, see, feel, hear, make in your life: material things, emotional things, spiritual, physical, family, social, mental, everything you could imagine, any want you could ever have, anything you could possibly desire during the next ten years.

The key is to do this exercise without worrying about how you can get it. Just let your mind go crazy. Take stock of all your dreams: new ones and the ones you've let go.

Remember that if you get something that inspires you enough; if you get a big enough WHY, you'll be able to find the HOW. Make sure as you brainstorm all your goals that they tie into your life purpose, because your life purpose is your WHY.

Step 2

Create a deadline (remember: a goal is a dream with a deadline). Next to each goal, set a deadline within which the goal must be obtained. Write '1yr' for goals you want to achieve in the next 12 months, '2yr' for goals you want to achieve in the next two years, '5yr' for goals you want to achieve in the next five years and '10yr' for goals you want to achieve in the next ten years.

Step 3

Circle all your one-year goals, and choose from them the four that are most compelling to you: the four that you would be most committed to achieving within a year. Make sure they are compelling enough to create tremendous excitement within you. Otherwise brainstorm additional goals.

Step 4

Having selected your top four goals, write them down on a fresh sheet of paper, under the heading 'Top one-year goals'. Under each goal, write down why you are absolutely committed to achieving this goal within the year. Sell yourself: Give yourself enough reasons to follow through, just as I did with my reasons to write this book. Think of the pleasure and the benefits you will get from achieving this goal.

Step 5

Next to your top four goals and your reasons why you want to achieve them, write down what it will cost you if you do not achieve them. What will you miss out on? What will you lose? Think of the pain you will feel if you do not achieve your goals. If I hadn't completed this book, I would have felt as though:
☛ I were letting myself down.
☛ I were weak.

☛ I would lose my positioning as a cutting-edge thinker.

☛ I would go stale.

☛ I would lose out on all the excitement that comes from writing a new book.

☛ I wouldn't achieve my turnover target for my company, which would mean that my personal income would suffer.

☛ My business partners would lose faith in me.

With all the pain that I knew I would feel if I didn't complete the book, I had enormous leverage on myself to complete it. I was willing to pay any price to make this book happen, including many 24-hour days and emotional strain.

Step 6

Choose a partner and tell them what your top four goals are and why you are committed to achieving these goals. Make sure that this partner is someone whom you trust, someone whom you know wants you to succeed, someone who can add value to your thoughts and ways of achieving your goals.

When I wrote *Lost and Found: My Journey to Hell and Back*, a lot of people told me that they thought I was very brave to share my experience with the rest of the world. I told them the truth: It had nothing to do with bravery. It had everything to do with talking about my experience so that I could get a clearer perspective on my life; where I had been and where I was going. Until you can express to other people what is going on inside your head, you cannot get absolute clarity on what it is that you want to achieve.

After speaking to almost 100 000 South Africans in the past year, I have discovered that the most difficult challenge for most of us is the ability to talk clearly and convincingly about our goals and dreams to other people. Start practising now. Get into the habit of talking about things that you were too scared to talk about before. Let it out. Your ability to talk about your dreams in such a way that even other people are inspired by them will determine whether they will help you make it happen.

In October 1997, I made the biggest goal in my life a reality because I had the ability to share it with a business partner in such a way that they became inspired to help me make it happen. My goal was to address at least 5 000 South Africans in a series of morning seminars throughout the country. These would be people who would actually pay to come and hear me speak because they wanted to, not because their companies had organized me to speak at one of their conferences.

It was my dream to speak at packed theatres like the Civic Theatre in Johannesburg and the Nico Malan in Cape Town, both of which have a capacity of more than 1 000 people. My challenge, however, was to get the huge upfront financial investment that staging a road show of this nature required. I needed a sponsor to help me make my dream a reality.

Nissan South Africa got me to motivate their frontline salespeople in May/June 1997. One night I shared my dream with some of their marketing executives. I pointed out that because their advertising slogan was 'Life is a journey. Enjoy the ride', they should sponsor my programme because that was the essence of my message: to get people to really enjoy the journey of life.

They were so impressed with my dream and what I hoped to achieve that they *did* sponsor me. They played a vital role in helping me make my dream come true. Without them, it may never have happened. Which just goes to show that if you can dream it, you can do it provided you've got the ability to talk about it passionately and convincingly to others.

Start your goal-setting programme. Have some fun. Let your dreams out and share them with others. Remember, as Shakespeare said, 'We are such stuff as dreams are made of.' Dare to dream. Dare to make the dream real. Dare to share the dream with others. Dare to let your own light shine.

The most important sale you'll ever make

Session Two

Understanding, aligning and redirecting your customer's beliefs

No one ever made a sale by proving the other person wrong

Remember the two primal forces that drive our behaviour: our need to avoid pain and our desire to gain pleasure. What we do in any given situation is based on our beliefs. Do we believe that if we do something it will lead to pain, or it will lead to pleasure? Our beliefs about what leads to pleasure and what leads to pain direct all our decisions, all our behaviour and shape our destiny. Remember that a belief is someone's internal truth.

Your beliefs about yourself and your life also ultimately determine your values, which are your internal guides that determine the way you live your life. If you believe that people are basically good and caring, one of your values will be trust. If you believe that people are basically evil and that everyone is out to get you, one of your values will be extreme caution. It makes sense that, in order to become a Master Persuader, you have to be able to identify other people's beliefs and values. Wherever possible, find out about the person before you attempt to make the sale. (Now is a good time to review the belief and value questions on page 52.)

Remember the questions that customers ask themselves before they buy:

☞ Do you really have my best interests in mind?
☞ Can I really trust you?
☞ What's in it for me?
☞ What do I have to give up in order to buy your product?
☞ What's the risk to me if I make the wrong decision?
☞ What will other people think of me if I buy this?
☞ What should I do?

These questions are testing the customer's beliefs: the level of certainty this person has about whether buying will lead to pain or pleasure. Remember that a customer must feel certain that buying from you will increase their pleasure and take away their pain. In order to make the customer believe this about you and your product, you need to understand and align with the customer's beliefs. The customer needs to perceive you as someone who is truly on the same wavelength as them.

One of the biggest drawbacks we all have is our desire to convince the other person that we are right. But no one ever sold anything to anyone by proving the other person wrong. If you fight another person's belief, it will just cause them to become even more entrenched in what they believe. No one likes to be threatened, contradicted or criticized. The moment we perceive someone else as a source of pain, we are driven to move away from that person.

Changing the cynical to the converted

Whenever I hear a customer express a belief that reveals their resistance or hesitation towards my service, I immediately align with them. I ensure that they perceive me as someone who not only empathizes with them, but as someone who shares their beliefs and who has their best interests at heart. I ask questions that cause my customer to refocus on other possible, desirable meanings that they can assign to me and my service.

Recently, I went to see the human resource director of a large public company. Although the human resource director agreed to see me, he immediately expressed his doubt and cynicism about motivators, sales trainers and all the services they offer. He said to me in a tone of contempt and sarcasm, 'Mr Lipkin, I have nothing against you personally. But I believe that all you so-called motivators are nothing but hucksters, conmen trying to get companies to pay good money for a bad service. I haven't had one good experience with people like yourself.' Phew!! I have to tell you it took all my discipline and professionalism not to lose it with this prospect. I felt the immediate surge of anger and resentment towards this man who had just insulted everything I stood for, everything that I had committed myself to achieving. Immediately after the surge, I felt the draining of energy as I was confronted by the full extent of his hostility. My immediate desire was to head for the door and the comfort of my car.

But my compelling reasons for selling my services to the human resource director forced me to stay, specifically the fact that he had a multimillion rand budget for training and development. Remember that one of my core beliefs is that everything that happens to me serves me. I said to myself, 'Lipkin, if you can sell this oke, you can do anything. Come on, let's see if you can do it! What a great challenge!!' Contrary to popular belief, it doesn't mean that you're not well if you talk to yourself, provided you say the right words. As I told earlier, I joke with delegates to my seminars that the main reason why I am always so motivated is that I attend all my own talks! But the truth is that I do walk my talk. I am constantly reminding myself to do what I advise others to do. The lesson I want to share with you here is that your internal dialogue during a tough meeting will determine your external dialogue with the prospect. If, when you are confronted with resistance, you say to yourself, 'Oh shit, what an idiot this customer is,' your words and your non-verbal language will reflect what's going on in your mind.

So when this prospect told me he believed motivators were conmen, I reminded myself that this was his internal truth. If I protested or contradicted him, I would merely reinforce that belief in his mind. So what would you have said in this situation? This is what I said to him, 'I know what you mean. Often, when I look at the people who call themselves motivators, I feel the same way. I'm curious about one thing, though, do you respect companies such as the South African Breweries, Deloitte & Touche and Toyota?' As expected, his response was, 'Of course, they're some of the best companies in South Africa!' I then continued, 'Well, do you suppose that if they were to use a consultant on a regular basis, that that consultant must be a person of substance?' To this question, my prospect responded, 'Yeah, I suppose so.'

At that moment, I took out glowing testimonials from those three companies and showed them to the prospect. As he was reading them, I said to him, 'You know, if I were in your shoes, I would've possibly had the same beliefs about motivators as you had *before* I arrived. Now, though, I'm sure you'll agree that if those companies believe in me so much that they use me on an ongoing basis, I'm an exception to the rule. Am I right?' Notice my use of words here: I classified myself as an exception to the rule; I didn't challenge his belief system; I didn't tell him that his rules were wrong; I positioned myself as an exception to the rule. His response was, 'Yeah, you're right. Maybe we can use you. In fact, when I read these letters I can see that there are some specific areas where I think we can do something together.' At that comment, I experienced instant sales ecstasy. You see, what I did was help the prospect suspend his disbelief in me and link a new meaning to what I stood for and the value I could deliver. The moment I succeeded in doing that, my prospect began to develop a new belief as to what was possible in terms of my contribution to his company.

The immediate consequence of my session with this prospect was that I invited him to attend a seminar of mine as my guest (this is also called 'free trial'). He was so impressed by what he experienced that shortly thereafter he commissioned me to complete a major project with his company. Abracadabra!!

The ultimate alignment and redirection of beliefs: winning a customer away from an established and trusted supplier

One of the biggest challenges facing any salesperson, marketer or businessperson is the ability to win a customer away from an established supplier. As I travel around the country, I constantly hear how difficult it is to pry someone away from a relationship where he believes he is getting everything he needs. Some salespeople resort to bad-mouthing their competition, which is like committing sales suicide. The moment you bad-mouth someone else, you lose credibility with your prospect. You lose your integrity and your dignity. What's more, the moment you criticize the supplier, you implicitly criticize the customer because you are casting doubt on their judgement.

Let's suppose a prospect says to you, 'You're a great person, but I really don't have a need for your product right now.' Rather than fighting or contradicting him, which will make him justify his current position, align and redirect his beliefs. Say, 'Well, I certainly envy your supplier – he must be doing one helluva job for you. Do you mind if I ask you just three questions?' Now, unless your prospect is in a really foul mood, he will say, 'No, not at all.' I have tried and tested asking the questions below successfully on a number of occasions. Try it for yourself and see what happens. Let me know:

1 **'Well, first, could you just tell me three things that your supplier is doing really well? I'm curious.'** What this question does, is allow your prospect to elaborate on things he already believes. And it puts him in alignment with you. Immediately, he sees you as an ally not a foe. Emotionally, you reassure the prospect that you are not a threat.

2 **'If there are three ways your service could be improved, what do you think they could be?'** By asking this question, you begin to redirect your prospect's focus. These may be three things he hasn't thought much about. I guarantee you, there's a good chance he'll think of things that could be improved. So you're also beginning to disturb the prospect or to demonstrate to him a need he didn't realize he had: a hurt.

3 **'If these unimproved areas continue to be left out, what are some of the consequences it will have on your company in the long term?'** What you're doing here is selling him the hurt.

The Abracadabra of aligning and redirecting someone's beliefs is to get them to tell you why they should change, not for you to tell them. The instant you tell them, you build up friction and resistance. When the other person tells you, it's true. When you tell the other person, it's merely your biased opinion. After asking the three questions and listening to the prospect's responses, ask the final, redirect questions: 'What will the price be if you don't at least expose yourself to other possibilities that solve your problems? If there's a way to avoid the consequences of those unimproved areas, it would certainly be important to do so, wouldn't it?' Now you've got someone who has a new set of beliefs, a new feeling of certainty. He's now learned to associate pain with not changing and at least the potential of pleasure by changing. Remember that we all have interests or desires that are not met. We all have hurt and pain that we suppress. Your mission as a Champion Salesperson and Master Persuader is to find both the pain and the pleasure and to stir them both up.

Remember ERBN, LRBN and DRAB

Your prospect's beliefs determine their emotional reasons to buy now, logical reasons to buy now or dominant reasons to avoid buying. The entire process of understanding, aligning and redirecting your prospect's beliefs is aimed at loading up the ERBN and LRBN and eliminating the DRAB.

(Remember: ERBN = emotional reasons to buy now

LRBN = logical reasons to buy now

DRAB = dominant reasons to avoid buying)

The most important sale you'll ever make

Session Three

State management: the difference between perspiration and persuasion

Are you in a constant state of grace?

The ability to manage your state, especially when the going get's tough, is a core quality of a Champion Salesperson. What do John Belushi, Elvis Presley and Marilyn Monroe have in common? Well, all of them appeared to be successful. They appeared to have everything any human being could ever want: adulation, fame, wealth, talent, charisma. Yet they were unable to deal with their gifts because they couldn't manage their states effectively. That's why they're no longer with us: because they turned to other sources like alcohol and drugs to change their states.

How many people do you know who have sabotaged themselves because they could not manage their states? How many people do you know who could not deal with their own success? How many people do you know who are inconsistent in the quality of their sales or business performance? (Are you?)

Recently, I was invited by the Sandton chapter of the Young Presidents Organisation, an association of men and women under the age of 50 who are chief executives or owners of medium to large businesses, to deliver a talk to their members. I remember the invitation that they sent out to their members because it summarized what success is all about. The invitation read as follows: *We are delighted to invite you to a talk by Mike Lipkin, South Africa's top motivational speaker at the moment.* Those three words, 'at the moment', say it all. You're only as good as your performance at any given moment.

One master characteristic that defines champions in any field of endeavour is their consistency of performance. They do not have an occasional excellent game, they have game excellence. They always perform at or near their personal best.

One of the best examples of game excellence and the absence thereof is to compare the performance of the Auckland Blues rugby team against that of the Northern Transvaal rugby team. The Auckland Blues never have a bad game. Even when they're slightly off the boil, they still produce the magic. Somehow, whenever they need it most, they reach deep down and find hidden reservoirs of brilliance. Northern Transvaal, on the other hand, are capable of a magnificent performance as they demonstrated when they were the only team, other than the national side, to beat the British Lions on their recent tour to South Africa. However, in the very next week after beating the British Lions, Northern Transvaal played so shockingly that they lost to South-West Districts, a bush league team from George in the Eastern Cape.

I have been motivating and coaching South Africans for almost five years. My biggest challenge during the first three years of my career as a motivator and coach was to sustain my performance at or near my peak. There were times when I was world-class and other times when I was barely professional. I remember how shocked I used to feel after a bad presentation. I felt like I had let my audience down; I felt like I had let myself down; I felt like I was losing my skills when I gave a bad presentation. I kept on thinking about my bad presentation long after I had delivered it; I seriously doubted my ability to keep going day after day, week after week; my confidence levels went on roller-coaster rides almost daily. Sound familiar? According to the thousands of South African salespeople to whom I have spoken in the past two years, the ability to control their emotions is their toughest task.

I think the difference between the mediocre and the magnificent is the difference in the ability to convert hard times into emotional and mental muscle. Magnificent salespeople make dust; mediocre people eat dust.

This is one of my favourite stories on managing emotions: Once upon a time there were two monks walking home from their temple. On their way home, they had to cross a wide river. Because they were both big, strong men, this crossing did not pose a problem to them. However, as they stood on the banks preparing to cross, they saw a young woman standing on the same side of the river about 50 metres downstream from them. This woman was small and slightly built. She was distressed because she knew she could not cross the river on her own.

Both monks looked at her. Monk A remembered his vow never to touch a woman and crossed the river without helping the unfortunate woman. Monk B also remembered his vow, but decided that helping the woman would take precedence over his vow. So he took her across the river on his shoulders and put her down on the other side.

The two monks then continued on their way. About two hours later, Monk A turned to Monk B and said, 'You should be ashamed of yourself. We both took a vow never to touch a woman and yet you carried that woman across the river on your shoulders.' Monk B responded, 'Yes, but I left the woman at the banks of the river about two hours ago. You're still carrying her around with you.'

Your ability to leave past defeats behind and free yourself of beliefs or rules that do not serve you any more will determine your future success. Very often, the only thing standing between you and your future is your past. If there's one reason why I have managed to sustain my level of success until now, it's my ability to turn myself on at will. I have learned that the master skill of Champion Salespeople is that they carry their own weather around inside of them irrespective of outside conditions. Champions have mastered the most powerful Abracadabra for winning: *You do not have to be successful to be happy, you have to be happy to be successful.* Happiness is an inside job.

There is no such thing as luck

If luck is defined as a piece of good fortune that comes to you by sheer chance like manna from heaven, I do not believe in it. I believe there is no such thing as coincidence. However, if luck is defined as opportunity which is drawn to the energy that invites it in, I believe in it whole-heartedly. Good fortune is attracted to good energy. If you are in an internal state of grace, you will become a magnet for the good things around you. Have you ever noticed how successful you become when you are in a good mood? Have you ever noticed how other people respond to you when you are in a good mood? Have you ever noticed how clever and creative you are when you are in a good mood?

Conversely, have you ever noticed how difficult life becomes when you are in a bad mood? Have you noticed how negatively other people respond to you? Have you noticed how physically sluggish you feel? Have you noticed how many stupid things you do and say when you're in a bad mood? Remember this fundamental truth: You are only as good as the mood you are in! Champion Salespeople are Master Mood Managers! They know how to click themselves into the emotional, physical and mental states that put them into a good mood! They have true power: they have access to positive energy as and when they want it. Do you?

The purpose of this session is to provide you with the quickest, most effective tools for immediately changing your emotional state in difficult situations so that you can maximize your personal, mental and emotional potential.

As a result of successfully completing this session, you will:

☛ be capable of identifying the two methods of changing your state instantly.

☛ create a series of power moves that you will be able to use to change your state from one of frustration or discouragement to one of power and enthusiasm.

☛ design a series of questions which will instantly change your focus to cause you to be in a peak state with all the emotional rewards that state brings.

The word 'emotion' comes from the Zulu word 'e-motion'

There are two primary ways to manage our states:

A We have to use our bodies to manage our state

We can use our bodies in various ways: the way we move, the way we breathe, the way we use our facial expressions and the gestures and poses we adopt as we interact with others. Any physical change in your body will instantly change your mental and emotional state. However, most people have not discovered the power they have to change their states by changing the way they use their bodies. Instead, when people don't like the way they're feeling, they eat, drink, smoke or take other drugs to try to improve their state. These approaches work in the short term but can be fatal in the longer term – just look at Belushi, Presley and Monroe.

By simply putting your body into a certain posture or using it in a certain way, you can instantly change and direct your emotional state. Emotion is caused by motion. Prove it to yourself right now. Stand up. Hold this book and keep on reading. Put a really, really sad, upset expression on your face. Pretend that you are about to burst into tears. Stand the way you would when you are really, really down. Hunch your shoulders forward. Look down. Breath in short, shallow bursts as if you were really anxious about something. Walk the way you would walk if you were really down. Stay like this for a little while. Now concentrate on your emotional state. How do you feel? Would *kak* be a good way to describe your mood?

Now put a huge smile on your face. Stand tall. Take a couple of deep breaths. Raise your right hand, clench your hand into a fist and bring your arm down in a dramatic, rapid movement. What's more, as you bring your arm down, shout the word 'YES!!!' at the top of your voice. Do this exercise again with your left hand and then with both arms together. How do you feel now (besides a little embarrassed if there's anybody watching you)? Do you feel energized and invigorated?

This was a simple demonstration to illustrate how much control you have over your emotions just by the way you use your body. By the way, how do you think other people perceive you when you are in a negative physical state versus when you are in an energized state? Remember: *The physical state that you are in when you are with a customer says more than any words you can ever say because 93 per cent of all communication is non-verbal.*

Use these four methods to manage your physical state for maximum energy and excitement:

1 **Develop power moves: explosive movements that make radical and empowering shifts in your state.** My move is the move I described above where I clench both fists and then pump my arms up and down while I shout the word 'YES!!' I can guarantee you that this works because I use it every day. In fact, I do it just before I give a talk or workshop. I don't have the luxury of taking time to warm up when I am in front of people. And nor do you. You make or break your sale in the first 30 seconds that you are in front of a client or prospect because they make an instant judgement about whether they like you or not. The next time you really want to wow the client, you'd better come out with all guns blazing. You just cannot afford to be in a negative physical state.

2 **Manage your breathing.** Very often when people feel intense stress or anxiety, they stop breathing, or their breathing becomes very short and shallow, so they actually feel like they are out of breath. Has this ever happened to you? When your body is deprived of oxygen, it sends an alarm signal to the brain. The signal reads: Crisis, Crisis, Crisis. And the body responds accordingly, which makes you feel even worse. If all you do is remember to keep taking deep, relaxed breaths during tense moments, you will manage your state positively. That's why the first thing actors and singers learn is how to breathe effectively.

Despite the fact that I have given over 500 talks in the past two years, I still get incredibly nervous before each talk, mainly because I make myself nervous. I know that if I am nervous, I've vaccinated myself against complacency. But every now and then, I get so nervous that I border on panic. Despite everything I've written in this book, I am also human. I also have my moments of vulnerability and weakness. That happened to me recently just before a major talk to the 500 most senior managers in the Altron Group at Gallagher Estate in Midrand.

I first addressed this group in 1995. The talk went extremely well. I was then called back by popular demand. I always find the second talk harder than the first because people expect so much more of you. You really have to stretch to meet their escalated expectations. What's more, the CEO of Altron is the legendary Bill Venter. Just before I was due to start, he approached me and said, 'I'm expecting great things from you!' That was all I needed to hear. I had an urgent need to vomit and shit at the same time. Ever happened to you?

That's when I took control and instructed myself to breathe deeply. I went outside, looked at the perfect blue sky and focused on the massive amounts of oxygen flowing into my body as I inhaled the crisp

Highveld winter air. I calmed down immediately. My confidence returned and with it my positive excitement about the opportunity to go out there one more time and knock the socks off Venter and Co. How did the talk go? Brilliantly.

Remember that the tone of your voice makes up 38 per cent of your ability to persuade the other person. Your prospect is listening for signs of either doubt or confidence in your voice as you try and sell you and your product. Have you ever listened to someone who was incredibly nervous and let their nervousness come through in their voice? What did you think of the person? Would you trust them with your money or your career?

3   **Manage your facial expressions: do facial aerobics.** Learn to laugh. Just the act of smiling and laughing can make you feel more energized. Try it now. Smile. Start off with a small smile, then make it wider. Now make it huge. Chuckle a little bit. Now laugh a bit louder. Now laugh really loudly. Don't worry about what the people around you think. We're all crazy anyway.

Have you noticed how infectious a smile is? When I deliver my sessions around the country, I have one really fun exercise: I challenge anyone not to smile at me if I smile at them. To date, no one has resisted the temptation to smile.

One of the first things I learned as a professional communicator and salesperson is the need to do facial aerobics before a presentation. What I do before the talk, in the car or in a quiet place, is to stretch my mouth in all directions; I stretch my tongue in all directions too; I make funny expressions and contort my face in the most outrageous ways. When I have finished, I feel as though my face is alive. My facial muscles are limbered up for great speech. Just like the rest of the body, you have to warm up your face for a presentation. When you talk, it's not just your mouth that's moving – it's your entire face.

4   **Develop a bold, decisive way of speaking and moving your body.** Especially use your upper body and arms when you talk and sell. If you move in a bold fashion, you will feel bold and the other person will perceive you as bold. Train yourself to be decisive in everything you do: Speak decisively, think decisively, move decisively, develop decisive gestures. Eliminate anything from your conduct that is hesitant or that could send out a signal of uncertainty. Eliminate 'junk words and gestures' from your personal style. Every time you murmur the sounds 'uh'

or 'um' or fidget with your pen, your ears, your hair, your nose, you are unconsciously demonstrating hesitancy or weakness. Remember the Champion Salesperson's edge: self-awareness.

The All Blacks' not-so-secret weapon

Just in case you've been sceptical as you've been reading through the preceding sections, let me ask you this: Do you believe that the All Blacks are a Champion Rugby Team? Patriotism aside, do you think that they're the best rugby team in the world right now? Do they consistently perform in an outstanding manner? Do you think that they carefully plan their moves for every game?

Why do you think they perform the Haka before the start of every game? Have you ever watched them as they do their Maori war-dance in front of the opposing team? Have you watched the intensity of their movements as they glare at their opponents? Have you listened to the lust for battle in their voices as they shout at the players facing them? What do you think their physical state is just before the start of the game? How do you think the other team feels at the start of the game, having just watched the All Blacks do their war-dance? (The best advice I can give South Africa, or any other team playing the All Blacks for that matter, is to either turn their backs on the All Blacks or to gather round in a circle, so that they are not facing the All Blacks when they do the Haka.)

The All Blacks know the value of getting into a peak performance state before each test match. They understand the edge it gives them from the opening whistle. They are 'psyched' *and* they have intimidated the opposition. Develop your own Haka. Develop your own war-dance. Develop your own 'psyching-up' ritual that gets you into a peak performance state before your own test matches. Give yourself the intensity edge.

Learn through OPE: *Umuntu ngumuntu ngabantu* (a person is a person because of other people)

Although I'm giving you a series of easy-to-learn, easy-to-apply steps to becoming a Master Persuader, the most powerful way to accelerate your effectiveness is through OPE: Other People's Experiences. Remember that success leaves clues. If you want to become a forceful manager of your body when you present, talk or sell, observe people who are already walking the talk. Model their behaviour. Do what they're doing, including the way they use their body. Very soon, you'll start to feel the same way they do. And you'll have the same impact.

I owe my early development as a communicator to a man called Darryl Phillips, chairman of the Grey Phillips Advertising Agency in the early to mid-Eighties. Darryl was a Master Persuader who had the ability to inspire both his own people and his clients with extreme confidence in his abilities. I openly admit that I cloned his communication style with powerful results.

I often find myself copying Reg Lascaris when I am listening to people. If listening is the most important part of the communication game, Reg is the game's grand master. He has the uncanny ability to become absolutely still as he single-mindedly focuses all his attention on the person to whom he is speaking. When I listen to people, I get an image of Reg in my brain and I listen with his intensity and his concentration.

One of the communicators I really admire because of his energy and spontaneity is Robert Brozin, CEO and founder of Nando's. When Robert speaks, he is incredibly credible because he speaks from the heart. He is real. He uses real words and he shows real emotions. I often emulate Robert's style, especially when I am talking to less sophisticated audiences.

I am also a great follower of an American motivator called Anthony Robbins. A lot of the material in this book has been influenced by him. I make sure that I attend at least one of his live programmes every year. Robbins has an explosive presentation style. He has incredible physical presence and he talks with electrifying decisiveness and energy. I often find myself practising his moves and experimenting with his style.

I take from the best and I weave their magic into my own. In a sense we are all strands of the people around us: *Umuntu ngumuntu ngabantu.* Rub up against enough magic and make sure that some of it sticks to you.

B We have to focus on the right things in the right way

The second way to manage our state is to change *what* we focus on and *how* we focus on the things around and inside us.

Having read *Lost and Found*, the book I wrote about my experience with clinical depression, people often ask me whether I really believe that depression is the result of a chemical change in the body. I tell them emphatically 'Yes'. But then I tell them further that every thought we ever have has a chemical reaction on the body. Think about it. Whenever you focus on an intensely negative thing in your life, you feel an immediate physical tension, your heartbeat goes up, your chest tightens, you feel a knot forming in the pit of your stomach, your palms become a little clammy, your breathing becomes short and shallow, you feel a numbness in your extremities, and so on.

On the other hand, when you focus on things that make you feel elated or excited, what kind of physical sensations do you feel? How about a slight warmth as the blood rushes to your cheeks? How about a burst of adrenalin as you think of the pleasure or adventure the thing you are focusing on will bring you? How about the sense of energy and buoyancy that good news always creates inside you? What about the long, deep breaths you take when you feel totally at peace and in control?

Just by thinking about something we create a chemical chain reaction in our bodies. Like you, I am faced with enormous challenges over the next 12 months. I have to make this book a success. I'm doing more and more work around the world, which is a massive challenge. I have to achieve all my highly ambitious one-year goals. I have to put myself on the line. I've probably taken on more than I should have. I could get very scared about what I have to do over the next year. There is a strong possibility that I may screw up big time.

On the other hand, I am blessed to have the opportunity to do what I'm doing. I've been given wings and I'm flying as high as I can. Every morning when I wake up, I cannot believe how lucky I am and how magical my life has become. My worst nightmare is probably somebody else's dream. Every day I feel like I'm growing faster than my four-year-old daughter. I have never felt so juiced in my life.

Why am I telling you this? Simply because I have a choice about what aspect of my life I can focus on. I am part of the same species as you: *Homo sapiens* – the Thinking Species. If I focus on what could go wrong, if I dwell on the downside of my life and all the pitfalls that lie between me and my goals, I will emotionally nosedive into a disempowered state. And if I can not manage my own state, how the heck am I going to manage my customers' states as well as those of all the thousands of people I get paid to excite every year?

The most simple and the most life-changing skill we can ever master is the discipline to direct our focus towards the magic not the tragic, towards the upside not the downside. If you were to ask me what my biggest challenge in life is and what it is likely to remain for the rest of my days on the planet, I would respond very simply: to remain focused on what empowers me, because that's the only way I can empower my customers and the people around me. I cannot give what I haven't got.

Have you noticed how seductive the dark side is? Have you noticed how most South Africans are not happy unless they're unhappy? Have you noticed that wherever you go, somehow the conversation always gets back to the bad news. From this moment on, start building your focus muscles. Resist the current that wants to pull you in the wrong direction. Whenever you find yourself getting sucked into the whirlpool of pessimism, listen to the alarm bells in your head. And force yourself to focus on the magic.

How I almost lost the South African Breweries as a client

Have you ever psyched yourself up for a major sales presentation and been totally ready to go out there and dazzle the client and then, just as you're about to go and present, you receive shocking news that knocks the wind out of you? That's what happened to me not so long ago.

From February 1995 until May 1997, I hosted a talk show on 702 Talk Radio. The name of my show was Power Talk. Every Sunday night, from 17:00 until 19:00, I would sit in front of the microphone and share what I called the 'mental technology of success' with my listeners. I loved that time. I loved being a radio talk show host. I loved the people who called in and I loved the profile the show gave me. I also loved all the compliments I received on the show as well as the delicious sense of anticipation I would feel every Sunday afternoon as I prepared to go on air. It wasn't the money that motivated me. In fact, I did the second hour of the show for free.

Then, 702 Talk Radio management decided to completely overhaul their programme offering. Along with a couple of other talk show hosts I got cut from the station. I heard about my fate from the programme manager, Alan Matthews, just minutes before I was due to deliver a workshop to the sales force of the South African Breweries at a conference in the Eastern Cape. Like people who believe they have been done an injustice everywhere, I was filled with a sense of anger and indignation. My ego was severely bruised. I believed I was the best of the best and yet my services as a talk show host were no longer wanted by 702. I felt as though my bubble had burst.

However, within a few minutes, I was due to motivate over 100 sales-people from one of the world's most turned-on organizations. I knew that if I continued to focus on why life was such a bitch and why certain people were so blind and stupid, I would sabotage my future by screwing up my impending sales and motivational session. I went through the 'focus-on-success' ritual (below); I used every focus muscle in my mind to get myself juiced again. The session went well and I still have SAB as a client.

The focus-on-success ritual: seven power questions

Just as we use questions to direct the focus of our prospects and customers, we can use questions to direct our own focus. If you ask yourself a question (like 'Why is life so unfair?') how does that make you feel? If you want to turn yourself on at will, ask yourself the following seven questions as many times as you can every day. Carry them around with you on a separate piece of paper. Get into the habit of focusing on them constantly. Continually come up with new answers to the questions and associate yourself fully with the answers:

1   What am I most happy about in my life right now?
2   What am I most excited about in my life right now?
3   What am I most proud about in my life right now?
4   What am I most grateful for in my life right now?
5   What am I enjoying most in my life right now?
6   What am I committed to in my life right now?
7   Who do I love? And who loves me in my life right now?

If you try to answer the questions and you believe that there is nothing that you are happy about, excited about, proud about, grateful for or committed to, just add the word 'could'. For example, say: What could I be happy about in my life right now?

I'll never go back down there again

After my book and talks on my recovery from depression, people often ask me whether I am scared of ever becoming depressed again. 'Never,' I tell them. This is mainly because I've learned to change my focus when I know I'm heading in the wrong direction. I'm not saying that I don't ever feel doubt or down. What I am saying is that I have disciplined myself to limit the amount of time that I spend in that disempowering zone. I have taken the advice of Forrest Gump, who said, 'If you're going to cry, cry. But do it quickly and do it alone.' In South Africa today and tomorrow, you cannot afford the luxury of a negative thought, especially when you're in front of people who are paying you to be there (or when you're in front of people by whom you would like to be paid to be there).

There is another very important thing that I've discovered about South Africans during my treks back and forth across the country: We do not give ourselves credit for what we have already achieved. We are continually underestimating ourselves. Remember this rule if you want to become a Master Persuader or Champion Salesperson: Always *overestimate* your ability. Put yourself in a situation before you're ready to handle the situation. Stretch.

When I'm faced with an unprecedented challenge, I focus on how I rose to other unprecedented challenges in the past. I focus on the successful end results of those situations to give me the confidence to handle my current challenge. The bottom line is that I've developed a deep confidence that I can handle anything, absolutely anything. As the late Vince Lombardi, the legendary American football coach, said, 'I never lose games. Sometimes I just run out of time.' In other words, I have ceased to believe in the notion of failure. All that happens to me now is that sometimes I get results that I didn't expect.

A final tool to get into a peak, empowered state instantly: your pre-meeting affirmation

Affirmations are worthless in and of themselves. If you walk around your garden affirming to yourself: There are no weeds! There are no weeds! There are no weeds! the weeds will take over your garden.

An affirmation is only powerful when it is in alignment with your purpose, your goals, your beliefs and your values. An affirmation can give you the final boost in commitment and energy to take yourself to the next level.

I have used my pre-presentation affirmation consistently for the past three years with outstanding results. I make this affirmation while I am in an intense emotional and physical state. It gives me a sense of strength, certainty and abundance when I need it most. It's like an emotional vitamin B injection to pump up my performance. Try it. Write your own affirmation and say it to yourself with passion and commitment before you see your next customer. Then try it again and again until it becomes part of your sales or presentation ritual. I would like to share my pre-presentation affirmation with you:

Mike's Affirmation

'I now command my subconscious mind to direct me in helping these people to better their life, by giving me the strength, the passion, the persuasion, the humour, the energy – whatever it takes – to get these people to buy into me and my message so that they can experience all the benefits and pleasure they truly desire and deserve. I will do whatever it takes and I will succeed in motivating them to buy into me now!'

The ten steps to sales mastery

Introduction

Wow! We've created a tremendous foundation. We now have a very good idea what makes people buy: People buy states. Your job and mine is to be an effective motivator: Somebody who finds a real want and ignites it, experiences it, develops a little hurt and a lot more pleasure. We've explored some of the tools of persuasion and the secrets of creating inner pressure to buy. We've spent a lot of time learning how to persuade ourselves so that we can persuade others in a deep and impactful way. If this were the end of the book, the application of the principles, questions and techniques that I've shared with you already could massively increase your powers of persuasion and sales mastery.

But Master Persuaders always go boldly further than their customers (or readers) ever expect them to go. My mission, now, is to take all the individual ideas and techniques that I've shared with you and organize them in an order that makes sense. I want to create something for you that you can do easily, quickly and consistently.

What I am now going to do is to give you an idea of the sequence in which the actions need to be taken. This entire book has been inspired by the thoughts and actions of the world's Champion Salespeople and Master Persuaders. If you are going to model or emulate champions, you can't just do what they do – you want to do what they do in the order that they do it. If you know all the right elements but you put them together in the wrong order and sequence, you will not get the same results. If you were provided with a recipe to make the world's most delicious meal but you were not told about the correct order in which to use the ingredients, it is unlikely that you would achieve the desired result. We are now going to put together all the elements in the sequence that will produce massive results.

As you immerse yourself in the fascinating principles of persuasion and selling which follow, remember that you won't always have to go through every one of the ten steps of sales. There may be certain situations that call for the application of just one of the steps. I'll leave you to decide when to apply each step. In the near future, though, you will have the opportunity to apply every single step. Spend time exploring all the steps, so that you have a complete picture of how Champion Salespeople weave their magic from A to Z.

Also take time to complete the 'salesplays' at the end of each step. They are designed to help you to integrate the knowledge and to apply it as quickly as possible. If you're really committed to being a Champion Salesperson and Master Persuader, you'll do these salesplays with someone who also wants to sharpen their saw. Buy some more books, spread them around and give others the greatest gift you can: the gift of personal development. (Notice how I keep trying to sell you more books. Also notice how I keep giving you very good reasons to buy more of my products and services. Are you consistently doing the same with your products and services?)

The three phases of sales mastery

The ten steps to sales mastery are grouped into three phases:

Phase one: engage them!

'engage: to occupy the attention or efforts of a person or people; to attract and hold fast; to attract or please; to interlock with; to entangle or involve'
– WEBSTER'S DICTIONARY

I love the Webster's definition of 'engage' – unless you can occupy your prospect's attention, unless you can attract them and hold them fast, unless you can interlock with them, unless you can entangle or involve them in your story, you cannot even begin to sell them on your services. If you cannot effectively engage the prospect as defined by Webster's, don't expect to get to second base. I meet so many salespeople in my sessions who moan about how hard the initial sales call is. They complain about people not being open-minded towards their products or services. My response to them is simply that they are blaming others for their lack of preparation and skill-deficiency.

Make a commitment to yourself right now: Whenever you don't connect with someone or whenever you don't get past first base, don't blame your prospect or their secretary or life or even God. Whenever you blame others for your lack of results, you give up your personal power. Simply ask yourself: What could I do better next time around? How can I use this experience to develop myself as a sales professional?

Let's look at the five steps to sales mastery that will make you a champion at engaging people:

1 Prepare and do your homework.
2 Turn on!
3 Make contact and get their attention.
4 Connect and become their best friend.
5 Create interest.

Let's examine how I managed to engage you in my attempt to get you to purchase this book. First of all, I did my homework in terms of anything that had ever been written on selling in South Africa. I saw that no book on selling has ever truly integrated the concept of what goes on inside someone with the actual skills required to persuade effectively. Then I got myself extremely excited about the potential for a book that could help people to develop themselves as human beings and not just professionals. After that, I made sure I grabbed your attention. I hired a public relations company to ensure that the book received extensive media coverage. And even if you didn't hear about it through the media, the eye-catching title and cover caught your attention. You see, in the business of publishing *and* selling, you *do* judge a book by its cover!

I know that I have connected with you and become, if not your best friend (only because we may not have personally met), at least a very good friend. I know that, by now, you are enjoying my style of writing and what I have to share with you. I know this because you have read this far. I am also confident that I have created enough interest inside of you to motivate you to carry on reading, because the best is yet to come.

Phase two: enlist them!

'enlist: to enter into some cause; to secure a person for some enterprise'

– WEBSTER'S DICTIONARY

During this phase you enlist the prospect to your cause. You get the prospect to buy into you and your services because they become convinced that your cause is their cause and vice versa. You develop a 'mutuality of interests' with the prospects. What you want from the relationship becomes exactly what the prospect wants from the relationship.

These two steps form the enlist phase on the road to sales mastery:
6　Qualify your prospects: probe for problems and magnify the hurt.
7　Create conviction and test close.

Think about how I have been trying to enlist you, to enter you into my cause because you believe that we have a mutual interest. I qualified you right at the beginning of the book: I told you that I believed you were already a champion but that you were sometimes frustrated because you couldn't find the right tools or technology to take yourself to the next level. Throughout the book, I have also been asking you questions that were designed to probe your problems and to magnify your hurt. I know that I have also created conviction inside of you that I can solve your problems; otherwise you wouldn't still be reading this.

Phase three: compel them!

'compel: to drive [someone] to a course of action; to secure or bring about by force; to overpower; to drive together; to unite by force; to have a powerful or irresistible effect or influence [on someone]; to provide a strong motivation or incentive towards a certain end'

— WEBSTER'S DICTIONARY

We all have favourite words. Here are some of mine: passion, energy, enthusiasm, excitement, magic, sizzling, connect, tenacity, champion, bold, triumph, courage, freedom, love, vitality, vibrancy, spontaneity – just to name a few. If you interpret the word 'force' in the definition above to mean 'my personal force', then I'm sure you'll agree with me.

Master Persuaders and Champion Salespeople have the ability to compel their prospects towards buying their services, products or ideas. Specifically, they take the following three final steps towards sales mastery:

8   Make it real and assume the sale.
9   Convert objections to commitments.
10 Make it easy and create a future.

Think of how I have taken these three steps throughout the book. Notice how I have continually tried to make the principles *real* to you. Notice how I have continually urged you to integrate these principles in your selling strategies as soon as possible. Notice how I have addressed your scepticisms and possible objections and tried to turn them into commitments.

In a sense, just by getting you to buy the book, I closed the sale. However, my objective with this book was to start a relationship with you. I saw this book as my way of getting to first base with you. I'll confess that what I've really tried to achieve, up until now and for the rest of the book, is to create a future between the two of us. Remember: *Anybody can make a sale, but only the Champions can make a customer – for life!*

Let's now explore each of the ten steps to sales mastery in detail. Get ready to fly!

The ten steps to sales mastery

Phase One
The engage phase

Step 1:

Prepare and do your homework

Preparation is power

How prepared are you when you walk in to meet a client or a prospect for the first time? How much do you really know about your customer in advance? How confident are you when you sit down in front of a client whom you know nothing about? How accurate are you when you shoot in the dark? How much does the prospect think of you when you cannot tailor your pitch to their environment? I believe that 'call reluctance', the reluctance to call on people to make the sale, is primarily the result of not being fully prepared. Call reluctance happens when you don't really know whom you're calling on, or what their desires are, or what objections they might have. Consequently, there is fear of the unknown. Remember that the more you know, you more confident you become.

Think about it: Have you ever had a meeting planned with a customer whom you knew really well? Weren't you excited to meet them? Weren't you confident of your ability to give them what they wanted? Did you not feel prepared to handle their queries and even their objections? Preparation is power. The purpose of this session is to offer you simple steps to prepare yourself to feel confident and strong in your ability to meet a prospect's needs anytime you walk in to a meeting.

As a result of completing this session, you will be able to identify and apply the six fundamentals of preparation that will be crucial to your success as a Champion Salesperson.

The six fundamentals of preparation

1 The first fundamental of preparation

Know exactly who the customer is. Anticipate their needs and how you can fulfil them.

When I call on a decision-maker to whom I want to sell my services, I do the following:

☛ I find out about the company. If it's a public company, it's very easy to get information. If it's not a public company, it can also be very easy to get information, as most companies today have a website that will give you plenty of information. Just this act alone – acquiring knowledge of the client's business in advance – will give you the edge, because most salespeople are not prepared to put in the effort of doing their homework on the client.

☛ I anticipate what their needs and wants will be based on my experience with companies in their industry. The key words here are 'in advance'. I know that this prospect will evaluate me based on his perception of my understanding of his business. Your customers do not want to educate you; they want you to educate them.

☞ If I know people in this prospect's industry, I ask them if they know or know about this particular person. I try to get a picture of this person as a human being, not just as a commercial decision-maker.

☞ I prepare myself to talk to the prospect in their language, for example, if I'm about to speak to someone in the information technology business, I will read about information technology before I see the prospect. Never underestimate the power of speaking to the prospect in their language: When the prospect hears certain key words, you could establish an immediate rapport. (Right now, you may want to go back and review the session on rapport.)

☞ If you are selling to a large company and there is the potential for additional sales to other parts of the company, ask for referrals from the person with whom you're already working. If you're doing a great job, they should be more than willing to direct you to other people in their company. When you do get a referral, ask questions about the person you are referred to. Ask about that person's challenges, strengths, weaknesses, likes, dislikes, needs, and so on.

☞ If your current customer is delighted with your service, they could become your biggest source of information on new prospects either within their own company or within their industry. This is one of the most underutilized sources of information in selling, simply because we either do not think to ask for it or we are too afraid to ask for it.

Harvey Mackay, CEO of the Mackay Envelope Corporation of America and a well-known marketing man, created a list of powerful facts that any Champion Salesperson should know about their client. Remember that the more you know about your client, the more you can customize your services to their needs and desires. And the more you know about your client, the more you can connect with them. Use the following points and build a database on your customers over time. Even if you don't religiously answer every point and keep accurate records, familiarize yourself with these questions and keep probing.

Once again, you could make a separate copy of these points and carry them around with you. Keep referring to them and keep getting answers to these issues. I guarantee you that having the information listed below will take you to places inside the customer's head that no other salesperson has ever explored before:

☛ Customer name (as well as nickname, if any); company name; home address; home and business telephone number.

☛ Birth date and place; home town. (Everyone always has strong emotions about their place of birth and home town.)

☛ Education: high school; university; degrees; sports played. If the prospect didn't attend university, are they sensitive about their lack of education?

☛ Family: marital status; spouse's name; spouse's interests; wedding anniversary; children; children's interests.

☛ Previous employment experience; previous position at current company; reasons for career moves.

☛ Customer's career: Is this person's career moving north or going south? What is the customer's attitude towards his or her current company? What are this person's medium- to long-range business objectives, both for themselves and for their company? What are this person's immediate business objectives, both for themselves and for their company? What are the key problems as the customer sees it?

☛ What is of the greatest concern to the customer right now: the welfare of his company or his own welfare? Is this person thinking of the past, present or future?

☛ Any 'symbols' in the office: degrees, diplomas, photos with well-known people, letters of commendation, family photos, artwork?

☛ Membership of professional, trade or social associations; special interests; politically active; active in the community; religion; subjects on which the customer has strong feelings; highly confidential items *not* to be discussed with the customer?

☛ Any mentors; what business or personal relationships does the customer have with other key people in the company; are they good relationships; which other people in our company know the customer; which other people in the customer's company are responsible for making the purchase decision; what's your relationship with them?

☛ Lifestyle: medical history (current condition of health); does the customer drink? If so, what and how much? Does the customer smoke? If not, is he or she offended by others smoking? Does the customer work out or play sports?

☛ The customer and you: What moral or ethical considerations are involved when you work with the customer? Does the customer feel any obligation to you, your company or your competition? If so, what? Does the proposal you plan to make to the customer require him or her to change a habit or take an action that is contrary to what they're used to doing? Is the customer primarily concerned about the opinions of others, very self-centred? Highly ethical? Rule-maker, rule-follower or rule-breaker?

☛ What are the priorities of the customer's management? Any conflicts between the customer and management? Can you help with these problems? How?

☛ Does your competitor have better answers to the preceding questions than you have?

I use Mackay's questions every day. I believe that this array of questions has been instrumental in getting me some of my biggest projects. The moment I know something about my customer that my competitor doesn't, I have an edge. What's more, if I know something about the customer that gives me an insight into the reasons why they behave the way they do, I adapt my presentation accordingly. The end result is a perfect 'fit' between my customer and me.

Warning: These questions will help you probe your customers for vital personal and commercial information, but you have to know *how* to ask these questions, you have to know *when* to ask them and you have to know *who* to ask. Sometimes, you have to wait until the client is ready to let you have information about themselves. However, if you get close enough to the customer and apply the principles you've already learned in this book, you will accelerate this process.

I know that I have achieved 'insider status' – once I have gained the customer's total confidence – when the customer reveals information to me that I know is sensitive or highly confidential. Once I have this information, I know that I have to keep it confidential. Nothing will kill you faster than betraying someone's trust or confidence. You have to become known as a person who never reveals his customer's secrets, especially when you are working with other customers in the same industry. Remember: Loose lips sink careers.

2 The second fundamental of preparation

Make sure you know absolutely your own product or service and the advantages and benefits you have to offer.

You absolutely have to know all the advantages and benefits your product or service has for the customer. You need to talk about these advantages and benefits with total confidence and total empathy with the customer's needs and desires. Remember that the more your product or service costs, the more convincing you need to be.

There will be times when you will not have been able to complete the first fundamental of preparation. This may be when you receive a call from a prospect who wants to see you immediately, or it may be when you meet a prospect on the plane or at a business or social gathering. The prospect may ask you a question about your product that shows he has a need for it. Unless you can respond immediately with your advantages and benefits, you may lose the possibility of the deal.

At least 30 per cent of all my work comes from people I meet at unplanned meetings: airports, business class lounges, planes, parties, business breakfasts, lunches and dinners, and so on. Because I have developed a profile through my books and tapes, people will often come up to me and ask me about my services. When that happens, I know I have a maximum of two minutes to tell them about the advantages and benefits of my service. And where do you think I get my inspiration for this three-minute personal commercial from? Yup, TV and radio commercials. From now on, look and listen to TV and radio commercials with a different perspective. The best commercials will tell you all about their product's advantages and benefits in 30 seconds to two minutes.

Salesplay: Sales script

Write the script for a powerful one- to two-minute presentation on your product or service's advantages and benefits. Share it with a buddy. Make a presentation to yourself in a mirror. Is your buddy sold on you? Are you sold on you?

I would like to share my two-minute sales script:

'I have researched the world's top persuaders, marketers and salespeople. I have discovered how they consistently achieve their outstanding results; what sets them apart from the crowd; what makes them so successful; what makes them different. My mission now is to share my findings with my customers. I help them design and implement the selling and persuasion strategies that turn their people into champions.

'Over the past year alone, I have worked with over 150 companies around the world, including the South African Breweries, Deloitte & Touche, IBM, Toyota and Nando's. I have personally enhanced the performance of almost 100 000 people. The main reason why I have made such a great impact on these companies and these people is that I help them go where they've never gone before. I help them to develop both the skills and the excitement to become the best they can be.

'I customize my programmes to the environments and challenges of my customers. I help them reach and sustain new levels of motivation, communication and bottom-line productivity. But you know what I really think gives me the edge in transferring knowledge to others: I make people have fun. People really look forward to my programmes because they laugh, they get excited, they play, they realise that business is a game, and that in order to win the game, you have to love what you're doing. I help them rediscover their love for the game.

'I know I can do the same for you. Have you got a business card? Here's mine. I'll call you in the morning to share some examples of how I have helped companies really turn their people on. Is that okay with you, because I'm sure you'd like to see your people turned on? Am I right?'

Would you be interested in hearing more as a result of my two-minute script? Could you get me interested in you as a result of your one- to two-minute script? Do you have a script? I believe that your ability to express the key advantages and benefits of your product in a short, powerful message will be another Abracadabra of new business for you.

I'll never forget my first job in selling: I answered an ad in the classified section of *The Star*. It was for a company that sold encyclopaedias door-to-door. I was 17 years old. I had just finished school and I would have done anything to get some money. Together with about 20 other greenhorns, I was put through a one-day training programme that consisted of four typed pages. This was the sales script that we were required to learn by heart. The script covered the introduction that would get you into the home, and the main sales pitch. All in all, the introduction was no more than 60 seconds long, while the main pitch was about two minutes. Although I was rejected more times than I care to remember by households from Secunda to Sasolburg, I made enough money in three months to pay for my first year of university. The number one lesson I learned was: Keep the pitch short, simple and sweet.

Oscar Wilde, the great British playwright, once wrote a letter to a friend, saying, 'I was going to write you a shorter letter but I didn't have the time.' Have you?

3 The third fundamental of preparation
Know your competition but never knock them.

It is imperative to know your competition but not to be dictated to by them. Be aware of your competition's initiatives, because their actions influence your customer's perception of you. For example, if your competition introduce new technology or ideas that the customer may find useful, you could instantly be positioned as obsolete or as a follower.

Be aware that your competition are always knocking at your customer's door. Many relationships and accounts are lost because salespeople start to take their customers for granted. Beware of the AAK that was discussed earlier.

If there is one principle you need to tattoo on the front of your brain if you want to sustain your performance as a Champion Salesperson, it's this: Romance and re-romance your customers all the time. Remember the words of the best-selling author Daphne Du Maurier: 'A great lover is not someone who has a different partner every night. A great lover is someone who makes his partner feel like a different partner every night.'

Be aware of competitive activities. If they are doing something extremely well, don't be afraid to copy their initiative, but make very sure that you put your own stamp on it. However, if you find yourself continually imitating your competition, you obviously need to increase your IQ: your **Innovation Quotient**.

Never, ever knock your competition with the customer. Often, a customer will ask your opinion on a competitor just to see whether you'll knock the competition or not. The moment you do, you cheapen yourself. Resist the temptation. If you really want to score points with the prospect, praise the competition and note the look of amazement in the prospect's eyes. Become known as someone who has only good things to say about people. If you have nothing good to say, just say nothing.

I have some outstanding competitors in the field of sales empowerment and motivation: people like David Molapo, Abner Mariri, Anthony Morris and Ian Thomas. Yet I know that they speak highly of me and I return the favour.

I have other competitors, however, I know bad-mouth me but, you know what? Every time they do that, my shares with that specific client rise in value. What's more, more often than not I hear about it and it just makes me more determined to outperform that competitor.

The fourth fundamental of preparation

Know all the potential objections that can come up about your product or service and have answers ready in advance.

Think about all the objections that you usually hear when you are attempting to persuade or sell somebody something. How about:

☛ I need to think it over.

☛ I haven't got the budget.

- ☛ I don't have a need for …
- ☛ I already have a supplier.
- ☛ You're too expensive.
- ☛ It's risky.
- ☛ I don't have the time.
- ☛ I need to speak to my committee.
- ☛ I'm not sure if it's right for my company.

What are the three most common objections that you hear? What are the most effective answers you can give? Practise these answers over and over again until you can answer them flawlessly with power and congruency.

The fifth fundamental of preparation

Expect the best and prepare for the worst.

Coca-Cola had an advertising slogan 'The pause that refreshes'. Kit Kat tell you to 'have a break' with them. I'm telling you: Rehearse your sale in advance. In your own mind, see the sale going extremely well. Visualize the customer buying into you and buying your product. Picture all the other people from the customer's company agreeing with you. Picture them nodding and smiling. Feel what it's like to make the sale. Go through the emotions of winning and closing the sale. Get excited as you see the customer signing on the dotted line. See yourself being irresistible. Consciously eliminate your doubts and anxieties.

At the same time, because you've completed the fourth fundamental of preparation, you are prepared for the objections that could arise. You see yourself handling these objections with elegance and confidence. You see the customer convinced by your words and actions. You feel the power within.

The difference between making the sale and losing it is often simply the willingness to rehearse the sale mentally. And yet, hardly any of the salespeople I meet practise this simple exercise. They are sceptical when I tell them everything is created twice: first in your mind, then in reality. Your thoughts are the highest form of energy you have. Whatever you think about most is what you become. So think about being the best darn salesperson that ever lived in your industry. Then walk your thoughts. Hey, what have you got to lose? Just try it. Develop those mental muscles, even though it may seem strange at first.

Remember that spectacular achievement is always preceded by unspectacular preparation, and what you practise in private will be rewarded in public.

The sixth fundamental of preparation

Create demand in advance.

As we discussed during the sessions on preframing and the law of social proof, Champion Salespeople are great personal marketers or advertisers: They create demand in advance of the phone call or the meeting for their services or product.

Before you've met your prospect, has he convinced himself that he should buy your product? Think about it. How many times have you seen an ad in the newspaper or magazine, on TV or heard it on radio and said to yourself, 'I gotta have that'? A great ad will do exactly that: It will create a demand inside of you for the product even before you've actually physically inspected or wanted it. Great advertising is why I run in Nike and Reebok shoes, snack on Big Korn Bites, aspire to drive a BMW, wear Boss and Diesel clothes, shop at Edgars, eat at Nando's and drink Castle Lite. I'm extremely brand conscious. I know advertising pays.

You know the word 'logo'. A brand's logo is the symbol used to advertise the brand. The Nike logo is the swoosh shape. The Adidas logo is the three stripes. The BMW logo is the blue and white symbol. The word 'logo' literally means 'meaning'. When you see a logo, you automatically associate a meaning with that logo. Your name is your logo. What does it mean to your prospect when they look at your name? Does it mean anything? Or nothing at all?

How can you do what the best advertisers do: How can you create demand in advance? Are there testimonials you can send to the client in advance? Are there referrals you can use? Are there customers who are so delighted with you that they may be prepared to sell you in advance to the prospect? Should you run your own direct marketing campaign by creating a brochure that you could send to prospects? Is there a creative way in which you could package your benefit to the customer and send it to them? We will explore some of the ways you can do this further on. In the meantime, remember: *Your mission and my mission is to serve people in such an outstanding fashion that they become raving fans of you and your service. They must rave about you to everyone they meet. They must evangelize your performance to others. In short, you must delight your customers to such an extent that they become your volunteer sales force.*

I told you about my presentation to Deloitte & Touche in Chicago, but I didn't tell you how I won that assignment. What happened was that I delivered a motivational talk to the Southern African partners of Deloitte & Touche at the Wild Coast Sun near Durban at the end of 1996. In the audience was a man called Jerry P. Leamon, who headed up the tax practice of Deloitte & Touche in America. He really liked my delivery and invited me to talk at a conference of his partners in Florida, America, in September 1997. In the mean time, however, he also raved about my performance to the folks at the Chicago practice. They decided to hire me on the basis of his praise. I owe Jerry P. Leamon big time. More and more of my work is coming from referrals: people who have been recommended to me by other people.

Think once more about how you can create demand in advance and get the law of social proof working for you.

The ten steps to sales mastery

Phase One
The engage phase

Step 2:
Turn on!

To achieve peak performance, you first have to reach a peak state

We have already talked a lot about the power of state management; the difference between perspiration and persuasion. We saw that many times, powerful people do not produce the results they want to achieve because they haven't managed their own emotional states. All human behaviour is the result of the state we are in at that particular moment. If you are going to perform at your best, you have to be in your best state.

This session will help you to take your state management to a new level. I want to ask you this question: If you could actually measure the quality of your state before you speak to a customer in order to maximize your performance, would you be interested in this technology? I am sure that your answer would be: 'Of course!' Well, in this session I will not only show you how to measure your state, I will also show you how you can immediately change your state to create peak performance even in spite of negative circumstances.

The peak performance state test

I'm sure that by now you agree that your ability to consistently get into a peak performance state is vital to your success as a Champion Salesperson. Answer the five questions below to see if you are indeed doing that (even if you are not a professional salesperson, these questions are vital: Instead of 'sales calls', read 'appointments made' or 'things I was afraid to say'):

1 Do you consistently measure your state in a precise way before you go see a customer?
2 If you answer is 'no', how much money have you lost in the last three years because you have not consistently managed your state? Don't exaggerate and don't underestimate; include calls you did not make and sales you never achieved. Also include calls you made but were not in your most powerful state to close, including call-backs you left out, and follow-up work you did not do. How much is the total that you lost?
3 How much has not managing your state over the last three years cost you emotionally in additional frustration, regret, anger, upset and lower self-esteem?
4 If you continue for the next five years not to manage your state, what will your future cost be? How will you feel about yourself?
5 If you were to consistently use what you are learning here and consistently manage your state – by changing your physiology, changing your

focus, asking the success ritual questions – right before a meeting with a customer, what difference will that make to your sales? How will you feel about yourself? How much fun would you have?

My ability to measure and manage my state is without question the main reason why I have been able to sustain my level of peak performance over the past five years. Just like you, there have been many times when I have been in a down state. I haven't felt motivated to go out and do what I know I have to do. I am not a machine. I also have my emotional peaks and valleys. Success is not the process of never feeling down. It's the process of managing your state and getting yourself to produce the quality of work that you are committed to – despite feeling down.

The key distinction here is that I identify my disempowering emotions and take action to change them. We have spoken at length about how to do that. In this session, I'll share with you how to jack up your awareness of these emotions so that you can measure and change them.

The mood meter

I have designed the mood meter to help you track your emotional states. On the following page you will see 20 emotions ranked from most favourable to least favourable with a score for each emotion. Obviously, there is an element of subjectivity in this technique. Any time you try to put a value on emotions, it has to be subjective. However, this device is based on not just my own experience, but also that of other champions with whom I have had the privilege to work.

This is very, very simple. You can demonstrate to yourself right now just how simple it is. Think about how you are feeling right now. Ask yourself which of the emotions on the mood meter you are feeling. Put the value of the emotion you are feeling next to the emotion on the mood meter. For example, if you feel passionate, put the value +9 next to the emotion. If you are feeling despairing, put the value of -10 next to the emotion you are feeling. If you are not feeling an emotion, leave it blank. Then add up your scores and get your mood value.

If you score 0, it means you are completely neutral, neither up nor down. You cannot score 0. If you score 0, it means you're dead. If you're in a minus score, it means you are in a disempowered state; you're cut off from your true abilities and skills. If you're in the plus category, you're feeling positive. The challenge is to increase your positive feelings and, of course, to get out of the negative zone. You can also see that I've included seven days on the mood meter, so you can track your mood value on a weekly basis. (**Warning:** If you find yourself in a consistently negative state day after day, you're in trouble. Take action now.)

The mood meter

Value	Mood/State	Day 1	2	3	4	5	6	7
+10	Ecstatic							
+9	Passionate							
+8	Elated							
+7	Delighted							
+6	Happy							
+5	Pleased							
+4	Determined							
+3	Encouraged							
+2	Cheerful							
+1	Satisfied							
0	Neutral							
-10	Despairing							
-9	Angry							
-8	Depressed							
-7	Anxious							
-6	Frustrated							
-5	Upset/Hurt							
-4	Miserable							
-3	Disappointed							
-2	Weary/Tired							
-1	Non-motivated							
Total mood value								

What's your mood value right now? Unless you scored +8 or above, you're not in a peak state. You're not ready to go out there and sell your prospects or customers on you. You're not in a turned-on emotional state, so how can you turn others on?

Go back to the section on state management and get yourself into a peak state. Change the way you use your body, change your focus, ask yourself the success ritual questions, do your affirmation. Ask yourself what it would take to get you into a +10 state. Then imagine yourself having those things. Use the mood meter again and see whether there has been a shift. Keep the mood meter with you at all times. Get into the habit of checking it and boosting your state or mood before every important customer contact or sales call.

Salesplay: Creating passion

One of the most powerful emotional states to put yourself in, if you aspire to being a Master Persuader, is the state of passion.

Get a buddy you know and trust. Let one of you be 'A' and the other 'B'. If you can't find a buddy, do this exercise by watching yourself in the mirror and pretending you're a prospect listening to you present. Do not give yourself an excuse not to do this salesplay. Don't be shy. This exercise will not only help you turn yourself on effectively. It's also a lot of fun.

☛ Let A talk to B about his or her product for one to two minutes, but do so in a state of boredom and apathy. B is to note in his or her mind how they feel during the presentation. B is also to note some of the ways A is using his or her body (for example, position, posture, gestures, facial expressions, and so on) and voice while A is boring and apathetic.

☛ After one to two minutes, A stops, changes his or her state radically, and becomes absolutely passionate and congruent in the presentation of the value of their product or service, again for one to two minutes. B is to note again how he or she feels during the presentation (that is, the difference) and how A is using physiology and voice differently.

☛ After one to two minutes of passionate presentation, A stops and B gives A one to two minutes of quality feedback about the precise differences in how A used his or her body and voice when bored versus passionate. B also tells A about the way A affected B's state or feeling when A was bored versus passionate. The purpose of this exercise is for A to understand which moves, expressions and tones create passion in the other person and which do the opposite. If you've been doing this by yourself, think about how you looked in the different states and think about how you made yourself feel.

☛ If you've been doing this salesplay with a buddy, let A and B switch roles and repeat the exercise.

The ten steps to sales mastery

Phase One
The engage phase

Step 3:

Make contact and get their attention

The more you make, the more you make

Many people in sales and marketing are well-prepared and turned on, but they still do not get in front of enough prospects. Selling only occurs when we make contact. No selling is going to happen unless you get eye to eye or at least ear to ear with the prospect.

However, it is not enough to just make contact. We have to make contact in such a way that we immediately grab attention, so that people want to hear our presentation.

In this session I will share with you the six vital ingredients of a great prospector, as well as the six persuasive, proven ways to make contact and grab your prospect's attention.

High-earning salespeople go out there and 'just do it'

A vital difference between high-earning and low-earning salespeople is their prospecting style. High-earning salespeople go out there and 'just do it'. They do it daily. They do it with intensity. And they enjoy it. They have a specific goal each and every day for the number of calls they are going to make, plus a minimum number of weekly prospecting goals.

The biggest distinction between high-earning and low-earning sales-people is that the latter just aren't talking to enough people to get good – let alone outstanding – results. If all you did as a result of reading this book is double the number of prospecting calls you made or presentations you do, your income would sky-rocket, and so would your confidence and skill levels. Remember what Woody Allen said: '80 per cent of success is just showing up!'

Did you know that the cheetah, one of nature's most well-endowed predators, misses its prey nine out of ten times? Imaging what would happen to the cheetah if it said to itself on the ninth failed hunt, 'Bugger this. I'm gonna become a vegetarian!' And yet that's exactly what a lot of us do: After a series of 'turn-aways', we become dejected; we lose heart; we let our spirit leak away.

Let me share my personal experience with you: Despite my skills as a Master Persuader, I still get turned away four out of five times on average. Many times, I don't make the sale simply because the prospect does not have an immediate need for my services. Other times, despite my best efforts, I just don't connect with the other person. Sometimes, although I've tried to turn myself on, I'm not at my peak or I'm jaded. There are many reasons why 80 per cent of the time I don't make the sale. But the main reason why I'm currently succeeding in the selling game is that I keep coming back for more. I probably make more prospecting calls than anybody else I know. And I make myself love it. Even when my brain says 'uh-uh', my heart says 'just one more'. You know why? Because I believe that the big sale I've been waiting for will happen on that call. And if it doesn't? I tell myself 'it just wasn't meant to be' and I carry on.

The six vital ingredients you need to be a great prospector are:

1 **High expectations on every call:** Every telephone call or meeting or letter or e-mail could be the one that delivers the massive sale. Believe it. You eventually become what you expect to become. And you sell what you expect to sell.

2 **High energy:** You've got to keep running. You see, every morning when the sun rises over Africa, the impala knows it must run faster than the lion to survive. And every lion knows it must run faster than the impala if it is to eat. So when the sun rises over Africa, whether you're an impala or a lion, you'd better start running, babe!

3 **Referrals:** Current customers can be the most lucrative generators of new prospects. Most of the Champion Salespeople I know have reached the point where over half of their prospects are referrals from current customers. I now spend very little time having to call on cold-call prospects without any introduction. Almost all my calls are either the result of a referral or at least someone who knows someone I have delighted.

From this moment on, try these magic words with a customer that you have delighted: 'I am thrilled that we have achieved such a great outcome together. It's been an absolute pleasure working with you on this project. I'd like to help an associate or colleague of yours achieve the same kind of results. Can you think of someone I could help create the same results as you and I have?'

At least 50 per cent of the time my customer will mention at least one name to me, and often more. Remember the supreme rule of abundance: Ask and you shall receive!

Even if you didn't sell the prospect, still ask for a referral: someone whom the prospect believes may in fact want your product or service. Remember that one referral is worth ten cold-calls. And the worst that can happen is that the prospect says 'no'.

4 **High, attention-grabbing impact:** Champion Salespeople have the ability to connect immediately with their prospects on a deeper level than their competitors. They know that influence over another person happens in a heartbeat – in the first 30 seconds to be exact. They have mastered the ways with which to arrest the attention of their prospect. Remember: *You are an interruption until you get the other person's attention.*

5 **Disciplined focus:** Champion prospectors have a minimum number of calls they know they must make every day. And they make them! They also have a plan for how they are going to make those calls – both face to face and ear to ear. They consistently make those calls day after day, week after week, month after month. They plan their work and they work their plan. They know that if they fail to plan, they plan to fail.

6 **Creativity and outrageousness:** In order to instantly grab the attention of the prospect and hold it, you have to be creative, even to the point of being outrageous (obviously within the parameters of reasonable taste). Ask yourself: How creative and outrageous am I when it comes to rivetting my prospect's attention? Am I a lightning and thunder kind of person or just a grey, ho-hum model.

What's more, if you are continually sharpening your creative edge, you stay vibrant and appealing. If you slip into a time-worn opening statement, you will grow stale from the inside out.

Six ways to grab your prospect's attention

It's all very well for me to tell you that you have to be creative and forceful in grabbing your prospect's attention. You're probably wondering, 'Yes, but how do I actually do it?' Funny you should ask! Here are seven ways to do just that:

1 **Smile:** It's sounds so simple but so few people do it. Have you ever noticed how tense people get when they're calling on someone for the first time? Well, practise self-awareness and smile – whether you are calling face to face, ear to ear or even writing a letter. But smile from your heart and not just from your face. As you are interfacing with the customer, remind yourself how lucky you are to be given a moment of that person's lifetime.

2 **Give a gift:** Think about how you feel when you receive a gift. I'm not talking about a massively expensive gift and I'm not talking about anything that could be called a 'bribe'. I'm talking about a small token of intelligence or fun that touches you on the inside. For example, knowing that I'm a motivational speaker, a supplier vying for my business sent me a small book called *The Prophet* by Kahlil Gibran. This is a book with deeply moving observations about our loves and fears. I was so touched by this supplier's thoughtfulness that I immediately called her and allowed her to set up an appointment to see me. She now does most of my printing work for me, and what's more, I've recommended her to many more people.

Let me tell you this amazing story: The most appreciated gift I've given clients cost me R26,45 each. It's a simple black T-shirt I produced, with the word 'Yes!!' in big white letters on the front and the words 'I can, I must, I will make a difference!' on the back, together with my name. I send it to prospects as a demonstration of my 'Just say Yes!!' philosophy towards life. It's a one-size-fits-all garment that was produced for me by my friend Myron Zaidel from Soviet Clothing. Almost every single prospect who received the T-shirt called me to set up a presentation for them. What's more, I now have all these people walking around with my name on their back. Hey, I'm trying!

It's not the financial value of the gift you send (in fact, if the gift is too valuable it may be returned to you): it's the emotional value.

3 **Make a big fat claim:** In the introduction to this book, I made a big fat claim to you. I promised to 'show you how to sell to others in an elegant, mutually nourishing way. I will show you not just how to make a sale but how to make a relationship that grows and becomes more valuable over time.' I trust that if you've got this far in the book, you'll agree that I've delivered against this claim.

Here are a few examples of how you can engineer the big fat claim into attention-grabbing questions:

☛ 'Sir, if we were to come into your company and save you 40 per cent on your payroll administration bill, you certainly would want to hear about the possibilities wouldn't you?'

☛ 'If there were a way to motivate your people so highly that they increase their sales by a third, you would want to know about it, would not you?'

I believe in overpromising *and* overdelivering. Make the big fat claim and then immediately substantiate your right to make that claim. Lead with your best shot. Don't wait until deep into the conversation or presentation to make the claim – by that time you've lost your prospect. So many salespeople take ages to get going. They splutter and stutter like a Model T-Ford before they get into stride. Make a big fat claim. Substantiate it. Be sincere. Be brief. Be seated.

4 **Create curiosity:** One of the most powerful emotional ways to grab your prospect's attention is to create curiosity. This is where the prospect says, 'Wow, that's interesting. I want to find out more.' **Warning:** Curiosity is an attention-grabbing device that requires huge doses of creativity. It is so powerful because it is so rarely done well and yet it is so simple. If you want to break free of the clutter of your competition and become a Master Persuader and Champion Prospector, curiosity will help you get there. Here are a few fun examples:

☛ From Toronto, Canada comes the example of a young lady who wanted a job with a specific advertising agency. She sent them a black box with a label on its cover. It read: 'Before, you've even hired me, I've started doing your work for you!' Now, if you were the person responsible for hiring, would you want to know what's in the box? Absolutely! Well, stuck on the inside lid of the box were the following words: 'To save you the trouble of crumpling up my CV before you throw it away, I've already done your work for you.' And, of course, inside the box was her crumpled up CV. Not only did this woman get the job, her curiosity device won an award for creativity at a leading advertising competition.

☛ From Johannesburg, South Africa, comes the story of a sales representative who was hungry for a big account. So she sent her prospect a Barbie doll without one arm and one leg. Of course, the card in the attached envelope said: 'I would give an arm and a leg for your business.' She got the business.

Both the above examples did not require big money to implement, just the desire and ability to generate curiosity in a fun yet relevant way.

You also need to develop a new description for yourself that grabs people's attention and arouses their curiosity. If somebody asks you, 'What do you do for a living?' what do you usually say? Do you say, 'I'm a salesperson'? 'I'm in insurance'? 'I'm in real estate'? 'I'm an accountant'? 'I'm a stockbroker'? The danger of answering questions this way is twofold:

☛ You risk the likelihood that these people already have preconceived notions about what a salesperson, insurance broker, accountant (especially) or stockbroker is. We both know that their notions of these professions are many times less than flattering, to say the least.

☛ It rarely grabs their attention. Have you ever heard anyone say, 'Wow, you're an accountant! That sounds unbelievably exciting!' or, 'Wow, you're in insurance! Tell me more; that sounds thrilling!'

On the other hand, what is your response when someone tells you they're a professional wrestler; or a member of Executive Outcomes, a mercenary organisation that hires out professional soldiers to dictators or despots who want to achieve outcomes in questionable climates; or a sports psychologist working with the All Blacks? You would like to know more, right? They've got your attention. Even if your profession is not as blatantly exotic as those I've just quoted, you can develop a new description for yourself that grabs people's attention and arouses their curiosity.

For example, a financial adviser in Pietermaritzburg describes himself as a 'protector of widows and orphans'. Isn't that outstanding? Wouldn't that get your attention? A highly successful real estate agent in Cape Town describes herself as 'a long-term pleasure provider'. An insurance salesperson in Gauteng, after some coaching from me, describes himself as a 'freedom giver'. His card now reads: 'Peter Gilbert, Freedom Giver'. Wouldn't that title get your attention?

I describe myself as a 'Master Persuader' and an 'Imagineer', which is a term that I borrowed from Walt Disney. Both definitions inevitably generate curiosity and discussion. I have even called my Company 'Touch The Sky (Pty) Ltd', because it is such an unusual name for a company. When people hear the name of my company, they always want to hear more. I've grabbed their attention. I'm in the door because I've separated myself from the crowd. I've created my own category where there is no competition. What's more, the moment I describe myself as a Master Persuader or Imagineer, I have to play the role. I become the label I've created for myself.

Remember: *If you can effectively and persuasively set yourself apart from the crowd in the mind of the prospect, you massively increase your chances of making both the sale and the relationship.*

5 **Surprise, surprise:** What's one of the rarest talents in communication or selling? How about the ability to deliver the unexpected in a way that surprises the prospect in a delightful way? Most of us have our noses so close to the grindstone that we can't see the real opportunities to capture the imagination and attention of our prospects.

Think for a moment about what has really motivated you to give your business to the people and companies you work with. Have you ever been pleasantly surprised by your supplier because they delivered the unexpected? How are you delivering the unexpected?

I'm sure you have heard of Nando's, the highly successful chain of chicken restaurants. Their entire marketing campaign is based on one fundamental rule: 'Surprise our prospects in such a way that they come to adore us!' That's why they run the advertising they do. That's why people talk as much about their advertising as they eat their chicken. Once again I ask you, 'How are you delivering the unexpected?' Are you the 'Nando's' of your industry?

I attempt to deliver the unexpected in everything I do, including in this book. I hope that by now you agree with me that this book is unlike any other book ever written on selling. Even the title was meant to surprise you.

In November 1996, I managed to persuade the South African Breweries to sponsor a Sales Mastery seminar of mine. The sponsoring brand was Castle Lite, because I'm the classic Yuppie and Castle Lite is aimed at Yuppies. No one expected a beer brand to be the sponsor of a sales programme.

Even my telephone messages are meant to surprise you. How do you feel when you call someone and you get their answering machine or voicemail? Mildly irritated, right? Well, if you were to call me on my cell number, here are some of the messages, you'd hear:

'Hi! Thanks for calling Mike Lipkin. I'm out motivating the nation, so leave a message and I'll get back to you. And remember, if, as you move through this world success would be your goal, keep your eye on the doughnut and not on the hole.'

'Hi! Thanks for calling Mike Lipkin. I'm out getting someone excited, so leave a message and I'll get back to you. And remember, the word 'fail' really stands for First Action In Learning.'

'Hi! Thanks for calling Mike Lipkin. I'm out energizing people, so leave a message and I'll get back to you. And remember, today is a gift, why do you think they call it "the present"?'

I change my message every two days. They always get a chuckle or a favourable comment. I'm walking my talk through the simple device of having an innovative voicemail message. Remember: *The way you grab the prospect's attention is what sets the tone for the rest of the relationship. In fact, if you don't deliver the unexpected, the chances are that there won't be a relationship!*

6 **Compliment, compliment:** I have a favourite saying that a good friend once shared with me: 'God gave me my relatives; I'll choose my friends.' I tell you that because unless you believe you're dealing with a friend in a prospecting or selling situation, you will never be able to perform at your best. If you don't believe you're dealing with a friend, you'll be cut off from the inspiration and creativity that comes from truly wanting to help someone you care for. My core belief about all my prospects, clients, partners and suppliers is that they are first and foremost my friends. If someone is your friend, isn't it easy to pay them a *genuine* compliment?

One of my personal rules for prospecting customers is that I will only go after people I like. Maybe you do not yet have that luxury. It doesn't matter; you can learn to like people. Learn to constantly look for opportunities to pay people genuine compliments in an innovative way, because everyone loves a genuine compliment.

I have found that prospects find genuine compliments very refreshing because they are given so rarely in South Africa. Furthermore, I do my homework on the client and their market so that my compliments are based on well-documented facts.

Another way in which I compliment clients – especially if they are listed companies – is to buy their shares and tell my prospect about this fact. I even send prospects proof of the fact that I've bought their shares, even if it's a small amount. By doing that, I immediately establish myself not just as someone prospecting for their business but as a stakeholder with common interests. I have done that with SAB, IBM, Engen, Investec and Altron, to name a few. In every instance, I believe it contributed greatly to motivate these companies to give me their business because I put my money where my mouth was.

We'll discuss compliments and building rapport in greater detail in the next session.

Salesplay: Make contact and grab attention

Take a blank piece of paper and write down your five most important prospects down the side of the page. Across the top of the page write down the six ways you know how to make contact and grab their attention. Then brainstorm how you can execute these six ways with your prospects. You can do this alone or, preferably, you can empower someone else to also improve their prospecting skills by doing it with you.

Ways to make contact and grab attention

	smile	gift	big fat claim	curiosity	surprise	compliment
Key Prospect 1						
Key Prospect 2						
Key Prospect 3						
Key Prospect 4						
Key Prospect 5						
Key Prospect 6						

Telephone power

No session on prospecting would be complete without an exploration of telephone power. For most salespeople, the telephone is their enemy, not their friend. Yet it is a powerful way to reach prospects and connect with them instantly. It can save more time, energy and money than any other tool available. Remember that 93 per cent of your effectiveness on the phone is your quality of voice: the passion, confidence, contribution and desire that can be heard by your prospect. Now, don't get me wrong: You can't talk shit and still be a successful prospector. The seven per cent of your effectiveness that words comprise is an important seven per cent and we will discuss it as well. But your telephone power will be fuelled by the emotions broadcast in your voice.

I'm sure there are certain people you really look forward to speaking with on the phone because they always energize you. And I'm sure there are others you really hate speaking to on the phone because their voice makes you depressed. And, if you haven't met someone, don't you also get a mental image in your mind of their face just from their voice? Well, how do people feel when they're talking to *you* on the phone? What mental image do they get in their mind of your face from your voice if they haven't actually met you?

The biggest challenge facing many salespeople is to change their misconceptions about what their purpose is when they're working on the phone. They are also not as effective as they could be because they haven't learned the fundamentals of telephone power. The purpose of this session is to define clearly how the telephone is used as a sales tool and how to be more effective in getting through directly to your prospects to set up appointments.

As a result of working through this session, you will learn:

☛ The key reasons why most people are rejected on the phone and how you can avoid that.
☛ The true purpose of using the telephone with prospects.
☛ The six keys to becoming a Master Telephone Persuader.
☛ How to get passed the secretary or gatekeeper in an elegant and effective manner.

Why people are rejected on the phone

These are the five biggest reasons why people are rejected on the phone:

1   Unless it's a planned conference call, a phone call is always an interruption in somebody else's day. Their instinctive response is one of wariness towards the caller.
2   The prospect is afraid that the caller will take up too much of their time.
3   The prospect may have many distractions while they are talking to you on the phone.
4   If the prospect doesn't know you, they may be suspicious of you. At best, they still don't feel a personal commitment to you.
5   Salespeople are often rejected because they are either indecisive or they try to achieve too much over the phone. They do not have clear objectives and the prospect can hear it.

The true purpose of the telephone

Unless you are specifically in the business of telesales (which merits a book in its own right), the purpose of the phone is not to close the sale. It is threefold:

1   To make contact.
2   To grab attention in a way that establishes mutuality of interest and rapport.
3   To set up an appointment or pave the way for future transactions.

The prospects have to feel like you are asking them to make a minor decision. They must not feel like they are committing themselves to an event of great consequence over the phone. They must feel zero anxiety and total anticipation about meeting you face to face.

The seven keys to becoming a Master Telephone Persuader

Here are my seven keys to becoming a Master Telephone Persuader:

1   **You must be in a turned-on state before you pick up the phone.** Put yourself at a level +10. Practise all the techniques that I have shared with you of how to turbo-boost your mind and body. While you are on the phone, stand the way you would stand if you were actually face to face with the prospect: Assume a bold, confident, relaxed stance.

   While you are speaking to the customer, *smile*. Have you ever noticed how you can hear a smile in someone's voice? The key to being effective on the phone is to have fun!

2   **Grab their attention immediately with the quality of your voice.** Focus on embracing the prospect with your voice. Use your voice as your outstretched hand with which you greet him or her. Your voice must relax and energize the prospect at the same time. As a result of hearing your voice, the prospect must be filled with a single thought: 'I want to meet this person.'

3   **Don't use the phone just because you need an appointment. Use the phone because you truly believe you are going to help the prospect.** You are a giver, not a taker. You have to feel like you have real value for prospect. This belief and this spirit of contribution will not only come through in your voice; it will also empower you to be at your most compelling. The only question for the prospect will then be *when* to meet, not *if* you should meet.

4   **Always ask questions.** Questions not only change the focus and state of your prospect, they also precipitate the law of reciprocation, where the prospect reciprocates by asking you questions.

5   **Make a big fat claim.** Grab the attention of the prospect by offering them a benefit that makes their mouth water. Make this offer in 20 seconds or less. You are not asking the person to buy anything or make a commitment. You are just exposing them to the big, fat, juicy claim you've made.

   Here's an example of a big fat claim and request for an appointment I make to a prospect: 'My company, Touch The Sky, has introduced a groundbreaking Sales Mastery programme that can increase salespeople's productivity by approximately 50 per cent within a three-month period of time. The way we do that is to coach your salespeople in an intensive, exciting two-day seminar and then follow up with calls, tapes and books. Some of the results we've had will amaze you! But what I'm calling for now is to see whether next Wednesday or Friday is better for you to find out how you can really increase the sales power of your people.'

6   **Make it easy and assume the appointment.** It's a very minor decision. Remember, the prospect is always busy when you want to meet them. If you are rejected, it's not because of you; it's because it's the wrong date. Always give your prospect an alternate choice. Remember the power of the double bind: Say, for example, 'Would you like to make an appointment right now or would you just like to jot down a time for us to get together? *Because* I'm sure the thing that is most important to you is creating the results you really want for your company. Isn't that true? So when should we meet? Would next Monday or Wednesday at 11 a.m. be best for you?'

7   **Persist: take at least nine noes.** Remember the cheetah. And remember that every time the prospect says 'no' to you, the greater the likelihood becomes that he will eventually say 'yes' because of the law of reciprocation. This is because gradually you build up a series of deposits in the emotional bank account. People usually do not like saying 'no'. If you persist in an elegant, pleasing way, you will eventually be successful. Handle any objections that may come up by aligning yourself with the person and then minimizing the objections. Ask for alternate dates once again. If you still get a 'no', call back the following week and then the next and the next and the next. Perseverance is a scarce commodity in South Africa. I have often agreed to see someone simply because of their persistence.

I'm sure that, just like me, you receive many calls every day on your answering machine or voicemail. More and more, the gatekeeper is being bypassed and the answering machine or voicemail is taking over. On average, I receive 50 calls a day on my voicemail. I return half of the calls, which are usually prospects calling for more details on my services. The other half of the calls are people who either want to sell me something or meet me to talk about a challenge that they have. I'll be honest with you: I'm so pressed for time that I don't return 80 per cent of those calls. You know why? Because the caller hasn't used one of the seven keys of telephone power. Do you? After reading this session, will you?

Rules of telephone discipline

If you are going to be a Master Telephone Persuader, you need to apply the three rules of telephone discipline with an iron will:

1 **Chain yourself to the phone and stay focused for a set time-limit.** Get into peak state and then sustain that state for your allotted telephone time. Remember that pure focus equals persistent power.

2 **Don't let anything or anybody disturb you.** Create a 'block' of time for your telephone work. Practise different approaches. Experiment. Become a master.

3 **To become effective, note the number of calls you make and the result of each call.** Keep a telephone log of your close ratios. Adjust and adapt your style accordingly.

How to get past the gatekeeper

One of the most difficult challenges in selling is to get past the gatekeeper to your prospect. Many salespeople fail to become Champion Salespeople because they can't even get to talk to the people who really count. I use these eight steps to achieve this awesome feat of persuasion mastery:

1 Make sure that the gatekeeper is your friend. Achieve this objective by learning the gatekeeper's name in advance and adopting a friendly yet forceful tone.
2 Always use first names.
3 Focus on really liking this person.
4 Tell them it's personal. This is always the truth: Anything that you want to discuss one on one with your prospect is personal.
5 Assume the authority. Let your confidence in the gatekeeper and her desire to let you speak to her boss come through in your voice.
6 Make it easy for the gatekeeper by minimizing the time you will require with the prospect. Here is how Harvey Mackay, whom I referenced earlier on, does this step: 'Hallo, Angela. I'm Harvey Mackay, president of Mackay Associates. I've written to Mr T in the last two weeks and I'm calling from Minneapolis. I'd like to see Mr T for exactly 300 seconds. I

will travel anywhere to come and see him for just 300 seconds. If I take longer, I will donate $500 to a charity of his choice, which I believe is the Boy Scouts, isn't it?' Now is that smooth or what? Who could resist that pitch? Is yours as good? Or even better?

7   If you are told that he is busy, don't leave a telephone number, call back or hold.

8   Persist, persist, persist.

Here is an example of how you might handle a prospecting call like a Champion Salesperson:

(Ring)
Prospect: Hallo.
You: Hallo – is that Bob?

P: Yes.
Y: Bob Smith?
       (So you've said his name twice.)
P: Yes.

Y: Hi, Bob, this is Mike Lipkin of Touch The Sky (Pty) Ltd. How are you?
       (Pause and check the prospect's state and availability at the moment.)
P: I'm well, thank you. *(Notice his state.)*

Y: That's great, Bob. Have you heard of me and what I do?
       (Again you are taking control of his mental focus by asking this question.)
P: Yes [or No].

Y: What I do is …
       (State big fat claim and assume the appointment: See rule 5 of being a Master Telephone Persuader.)

Salesplay: Master telephone persuader

1   Prepare your own script for setting up appointments and overcoming objections. Make sure you have a big fat juicy claim that you can substantiate. And make sure you can communicate your big fat claim in 20 seconds or less. Practise it.

2   Prepare your own script for getting past the gatekeeper. Practise it.

The ten steps to sales mastery

Phase One

The engage phase

Step 4:

Connect and become their best friend

It's not about closing – it's about bonding

All over the world the Champion Salespeople that I've researched say that the most important aspect of persuasion and selling is not closing – it's bonding. ***Trust between the salesperson and the prospect is the most important element that will influence the success or failure of a sales interview.*** (Think about your own buying behaviour, especially when a large amount of money is at stake.) Affection between the salesperson and the prospect is the second most important element. If there is not mutual affection between customer and salesperson, there is not a chance for a viable long-term relationship.

People often buy products they may not even need from salespeople if they really like them. This is true both in a personal and commercial sense. We all know that if a commercial buyer has the budget, and he can generate a logical explanation for the purchase of a certain product or service, he will go ahead and buy it.

I have personally experienced this phenomenon many times. One of the products I sell in my range of offering is the 'Yes!!' T-shirt. Often, I will attempt to persuade the buyer to acquire T-shirts for his people as part of the whole package that I deliver to his company. The T-shirts are nothing more than a 'nice-to-have'. However, if I have bonded strongly with the customer and they have the budget, I usually manage to make the incremental sale.

Even if you are not the greatest presenter in the world, but you have bonded with the client on an emotional level and you have a decent product to sell that meets the client's requirements, the client will even assist you in closing the sale if they really like you.

Furthermore, if a customer is faced with competitive offerings which all meet their needs and/or wants, they will go with the supplier who has managed to generate the best chemistry between them. If a prospect believes in you and the calibre of relationship they expect to enjoy with you in the future, they will put their money where their expectations are.

The purpose of this session, therefore, is to remind you of what you already know, as well as to introduce you to highly effective new skills that can help you to create a stronger bond with the prospect immediately. Remember: ***The ultimate goal of any Champion Salesperson is to turn your prospect into your friend.*** This is for two primary reasons: Firstly, as we have already seen, it is much easier to hire a friend than someone you do not like; and secondly, it's much harder to fire a friend than someone you do not like.

As a result of completing this session, you will:

☛ develop the habit of focusing on the things you like about people the moment you meet them.

☛ learn ten ways to give effective and sincere compliments that break the ice and build rapport.

☛ practise and begin mastering systems for creating immediate subliminal rapport through 'matching and mirroring'.

Remember: *The number one question we all ask ourselves when we are face to face with anyone who is trying to persuade us: Do you really have my best interests in mind?*

Have you ever been into a clothing store and watched someone try on clothes that obviously do not flatter them, and yet you hear the salesperson say to them, 'Yes, that suit is definitely you. You look fabulous. Will that be account or cash?' Have you ever had anyone try to sell something to you when you believed they only cared about the commission or profit they'll make on the deal? Am I right in saying that you not only distrusted these people as a result of their behaviour, but that you began to dislike them at the same time?

Champion Salespeople, therefore, start every encounter with a single-minded self-directed challenge: *How can I do what's best for this person in such a way that I generate trust and affection between us while I make an acceptable profit for myself?*

I promise you that if you tattoo this question on to your brain every time you go face to face with your prospects, you will become a 'trust and affection inducer' and your sales will rocket. I've got to the point where I actually verbalize this mission to the prospect. I'm not *skaam* to say anything anymore.

I have discovered that people love people who are spontaneous. They love people who are able to be themselves. They love people who are open. The sooner you can prove that you are all these things, the sooner you will generate mutual trust and affection.

Be kind to strangers – go for the magic!

Be kind to strangers, because you never know when you're entertaining an angel. You never know who is watching. And you never know what could happen as a result of this encounter.

When you meet people for the first time, what's your immediate instinct? Are you cautious? Do you judge them immediately? Are they guilty until they prove themselves innocent? Do you radiate a sense of joy and delight at meeting them or are you so wrapped up in your *kak* that you're not even thinking about the other person? Do you go for the tragic in them – do you look to criticize them? Or do you go for the magic in them – do you look to celebrate them?

When two Tibetans meet each other, they place their palms together with their fingers facing skyward and they say their greeting: 'I honour the greatness in you!' My wish in writing in this book is that I can persuade you to honour the greatness in everyone you meet, even if that person has different values to you or comes from a very different culture. Don't judge – celebrate.

You never know who is watching you

I would like to share one of my favourite experiences with you: Recently, I was at Durban International Airport about to board an SAA flight to Johannesburg. It was 17:00 and the flight was due to leave at 18:00. I was the twelfth passenger in the business class queue. Just then, we heard the four most feared words in the English language: 'the computer went down'. Well, as you can imagine, the passengers began to get pretty irritated. They started to shout at the ground hostess, Farida. But she was awesome: The more they shouted at her, the calmer she got. She smiled at them, told them to leave their baggage with her and go to the business class lounge where she would bring them their boarding passes when the computer came back on line.

When I approached Farida, I said to her, 'Farida, I just want to tell you that I think you're amazing. I watched you handle all those irate passengers with courtesy and elegance. You didn't lose your cool even once. You're an inspiration to me. Thank you!' Well, Farida just gave me this big smile and her eyes moistened with emotion as she managed to whisper her gratitude for the compliment to me.

Why am I telling you this story? Because standing directly behind me was a man called Albert Jordaan, financial director of the CSIR. I didn't know he was standing there until three weeks later when I received a call from Geoff Garrett, president of the CSIR. This is what Geoff said to me on the phone, 'Mike, would you be interested in motivating about 500 physicists, scientists, biologists and engineers?' 'Definitely,' I replied, following up with a question, 'Geoff, may I ask why you're calling me?' His response amazed me: 'Mike,' he said, 'to be honest I wasn't even aware of you until three weeks ago when my financial director told me about you. He said he stood behind you and observed you motivate a ground hostess almost to tears in less than a minute. And I said to myself, if he can motivate a ground hostess, he can motivate scientists and engineers.'

I have since done lots of work for the CSIR worth thousands of rands. What's my point? Simply to go for the magic in everyone because you never know who is watching and when it's going to be worth thousands of rands to you!

Remember the law of reciprocation: If you go for the magic in others they will go for the magic in you. Train yourself to consistently focus on what's outstanding about the other person. Keep asking yourself these three questions about everyone you meet:

☞ Why is this person magnificent?
☞ Why should I love this person?
☞ What can I learn from this person?

I believe that people don't care how much you know until they know how much you care. This is what I say to all the thousands of people I address in my seminars every year: 'Don't be like me. I'm an emotional exhibition-ist and psychological flasher. That's my style. I am purposefully outrageous and controversial. You have to discover and develop your own style. If you are softly spoken and quiet, that's fine. If you are loud and brash, that's also fine. Just remember two things: Adapt your style as much as you can to the person to whom you are selling and make sure that the other person knows your level of passion for your product and love for them personally. Don't be afraid to tell people how much you like them or enjoy doing business with them.'

The most powerful Champion Salespeople are the ones who have learned to care deeply for people they've just met. Then they develop and demonstrate their level of caring for their customers over time.

The fine art of compliments

We've discussed the power of compliments throughout this book. Now, I'll share with you how Master Persuaders apply this fine art.

Compliments create a very real power to bond. Everyone wants to feel appreciated. We all want to feel special. Mary Kay Ash, the lady who founded the massive cosmetics company in America, Mary Kay Cosmetics, advises her salespeople: 'When you are selling to a prospect, pretend that they have a big sign around their neck that says "Please make me feel spe-cial."' A compliment has the power to make someone feel special more than almost anything else you can do.

Warning: There is a huge difference between a sincere compliment, genuinely given, and idle flattery that is meant to manipulate. Idle flattery has the potential to damage your connection with the other person irreversibly because it betrays your lack of integrity or sensitivity to the other person. At best, idle flattery will annoy the prospect or customer because it gives the impression that you're trying too hard.

In order to give an effective compliment, you need to do three things:

☛ Tell the client what you like about them or what they have achieved. Make sure you really mean it. Be congruent.

☛ Justify the compliment by saying: 'That is because…'

☛ Ask a question about what you just stated; a question which shows even more interest: 'What is it that you do to make you so effective in that area?' In this way, not only do you get to pay an effective compliment, you also get to learn something.

I recently paid this compliment to a client I believed was outstanding at building team spirit within his company: 'Neill, I really admire the way you've built a winning team in this company. That's because I can see how excited all your people are to work together and how much trust they have for each other. What is it you do that makes you so effective at bringing people together?' Needless to say, Neill felt great and I learned another tip on motivating people. (By the way, in Neill's case it was his ability to remain absolutely fair and consistent in the way he handled everyone in his company. He had a group of really turned-on, educated, young people who were all self-starters. He saw his role primarily as an umpire and a coach, not as a manager.)

Ten effective ways to use compliments

There are ten extremely effective ways to use compliments that can build not only your sales career, but also support the people around you in feeling incredibly appreciated and loved. These are:

1 Make compliments a habit. Programme yourself to pay compliments at every appropriate moment. At the end of every day, complete your compliment audit: ask yourself whether you've paid at least ten compliments that day.

2 Continually ask yourself questions: What do I like/admire/celebrate about this person or company?

3 Give third-party compliments: I was talking to John the other day and you should hear the great things he says about you.

4   Compliment people to other people you meet. It will get back to them.
5   Give someone a compliment about something that means a lot to them. Complimenting people about meaningful things has more power than complimenting people about things they do not really care about.
6   Don't tell a person what you like unless you really like it: insincerity offends.
7   Compliment everyone. Everyone has something unique and admirable. Find it.
8   Don't just compliment the obvious. Everyone does that. Find interesting, hidden things to compliment that you know mean a lot to the client.
9   Compliment people in a way that they want to be complimented. For example, if there is a person who hates being in the limelight, don't make your compliment so loud or obtrusive that everyone turns to look.
10 Send 'thank you' notes that are complimentary. Some of my most treasured literature is complimentary letters from delighted clients with whom I've worked.

Salesplay: Care and compliment

☞ Design three questions you can ask yourself about virtually anyone that will cause you to begin caring about them on a deeper level. Use these questions to get into a state of caring for the other person. They'll feel it.

☞ In the next three hours (unless you're reading this in bed and are about to go to sleep), give three different compliments to three different people. Remember that, for a compliment to be effective, you have to state something you like, justify why you like it and ask a question about it. Try it now and enjoy the results.

The magic of matching and mirroring

In the session on the first master tool of persuasion, rapport, we briefly discussed the concept of 'matching and mirroring'. We'll now explore this powerful tool of persuasion further so that you can learn to apply it in your quest to become a Champion Salesperson.

Have you ever had the experience that someone felt that you didn't care for them despite the fact that you cared for them deeply? How many times has someone felt that you weren't enthusiastic about something whereas in fact you really were? How many times have you thought that someone wasn't really interested in what you were saying whereas in fact they were? How many times have you thought that you didn't connect with someone whereas you really did? Often, right?

Many times, the reason why these misunderstandings occur is that people do not match and mirror each other. By that I mean that they do not reflect how much they like or *are like* the other person. Who are the people you like best? I guarantee you that they are either people who are like you or how you would like to be. We even tend to marry people who look like us. (*Cosmopolitan* magazine recently featured an article called 'Facial attraction' which explored this.) We buy dogs that reflect our personalities and looks (think about Winston Churchill and his bulldog). We like being with people who share our values and outlook on life (that's why we like being with friends and family).

It makes sense that the more you can demonstrate how similar you are to another person, the more they will respond to you and trust you. The most effective way in which you can achieve this alignment is through the process of matching and mirroring. I guarantee you that if you can learn to use your words, your voice and your body in an effective way, you'll be able to influence and connect with almost anybody. This is not manipulation. I hate that word. Manipulation is using another person with no regard for that person's well-being. My central theme throughout this book is the absolute need to add value to the other person: to get what you want by helping the other person get what they want. Let's look at how you can use your words, your voice and your body to demonstrate how similar you are to the other person and to connect deeply with them.

Words: what senses does your customer use to process their world?

This is a really fun part of the matching process. It's also extremely simple. All you have to do is listen to the kind of words the other person uses. Study the key trigger words of their industry. Review the section on rapport again. Start practising using the client's terminology. Listen to the words that they use when they are really excited. Listen to the words that they use to describe what they like the most. Keep a record of these words. And use them when you want to persuade the client to your point of view.

What is really vital, though, is to listen to what senses your customer uses primarily to process their world: Is it seeing, hearing or touching? For example, if you hear the client saying, 'I see what you mean' or 'I can't picture that' or 'Here's my vision for the project', you know they are primarily visual. However, if your client says, 'I hear what you're saying' or 'That sounds good' or 'It rings a bell', you know they are primarily auditory. If, on the other hand, you hear them say, 'I just can't get a handle on this' or 'This just doesn't feel good to me' or 'I can't come to grips with this', you know they are primarily feeling or kinesthetic.

All of us obviously use all three modes, but we do tend to have one dominant mode. Once you discover what your customer's dominant mode is, play to it. Keep in mind that the dominant mode may change depending on the situation. Obviously, if you are selling a visual object, you need to use visual terms. But, as a rule, listen for the client's dominant mode and then get into that dominant mode as often as possible.

Voice

Your voice is a powerful matching tool. Aspects of your voice to match your customer's voice are:

- ☛ **Volume:** If the customer talks loudly, match him or her; if the customer is softly spoken, lower the volume of your voice. (Obviously, if the customer is shouting in anger, don't take your volume to that level!)
- ☛ **Tempo:** If the customer talks fast, match him or her; if the customer speaks slowly, slow down your tempo.
- ☛ **Tone:** If the customer's tone is firm, brisk and formal, use the same tone. If they are playful and light-hearted, match it. (However, if the customer's tone is tense and angry, don't match it!)
- ☛ **Timbre:** If the customer has a deep voice, deepen yours. If they have a higher pitched timbre, raise yours.

Body

Aspects of your body to mirror the customer are:

- ☛ **Posture:** Mirror the client's posture, except when they are in a negative mindset: Then you job is to energize them.
- ☛ **Movements:** Watch the way your client moves his or her body and mirror them.
- ☛ **Gestures and facial expressions:** Mirror the client's positive gestures and facial expressions but obviously not in a blatant way.
- ☛ **Eye contact:** This is an area that has been discussed by many presentation experts. I believe that you should make eye contact with the client

but don't make eye contact to the point where it becomes uncomfortable. Be guided by your client. If your client is the kind of person who enjoys lots of eye contact then give it to her or him. If not, back off a little.

☛ **Breathing:** Mirror the client's breathing pattern – you'll be amazed at the alignment that you generate.

☛ **Space:** Observe the client's space preferences. Some clients need lots of space around them, some very little. Never crowd your client. Have you ever been with someone who stands too close to you? Doesn't it bug you? Don't commit this relationship error.

☛ **Touching:** Some clients like to be touched, others not. If the client touches you, then you know it's okay. Wait for the client's signal.

The two final rules of matching and mirroring are:

☛ **Start off at the other person's pace and style.** Then you can change the pace slightly and they'll follow you. But you have to establish the bonding upfront. You have to earn the right to lead and be trusted.

☛ **Be flexible.** Flexibility is power. The person who has the most flexibility, the most choices, will control the situation.

Salesplay: Mirroring and matching

Think of your ten most important customers and prospects right now. Think about what their most dominant sense is. Think about how you could use your words, voice and body to match and mirror them.

Start applying this powerful concept with those ten people as soon as possible.

The ten steps to sales mastery

Phase One

The engage phase

Step 5:

Create interest

You have to make your customer hungry for more: how to make anyone interested in you and your service

One of the major mistakes many salespeople make is jumping into their presentation on their product or service before they've made the customer or prospect truly interested in hearing it. This could be a waste of time. The key to making a Champion Sales Presentation is to get your prospect hungry for more before you try and make the actual sale.

The key to raising interest levels is to ask questions that will focus the prospect's attention on desires that are not being met and the consequences or problems arising from that fact. Remember the need to stir up and heal the hurt, because if they don't think there's a problem, there is no need for a solution (which is what your product needs to be). Your mission as a Champion Salesperson is to make the prospect's problems and dissatisfaction clear and to bring it into focus in their mind.

The way to create stronger interest in the mind of the prospect about your product is to describe their problems back to them in detail. The more you talk of their problem, the more you must convince them of their need for your solution. Again, instead of trying to grab interest just by talking, grab interest by asking strong questions (review the session on the second master tool of persuasion: questions).

When you ask a question that forces the prospect to think and reply, it creates a two-way conversation and shifts the pressure away from you. When you focus on the hurt associated with what the prospect is missing, you will always deepen their interest. The challenge is to create *units of interest* in the mind of the prospect.

The purpose of this session is to share with you a six-step formula that will help get the prospect hungry to hear your presentation and answer your questions. If the prospect isn't hungry, they're not going to feast on your product or service.

I guarantee you that if you can master this six-step formula, you will be able to create extreme interest in almost everyone you meet.

The six-step formula for creating units of interest

I want to share with you the formula I use to sell people on my seminars:

Step 1: **State a BIG FAT CLAIM.**
Example: 'I can help you to increase your sales and productivity from 30 per cent to 300 per cent!'

It has to be a big fat claim that the prospect really believes is valuable. The response of the customer must be 'Wow!' And it must be a claim you can back up.

Step 2:   **BECAUSE – State a feature.**
Example: 'Because what I teach in my programmes are ground-breaking sales and persuasion techniques modelled on the world's master persuaders and salespeople. South Africans have never been exposed to these techniques before.'
Here I back up the big fat claim with a fact. The word I use in this transition is 'because'.

Step 3:   **WHICH MEANS TO YOU – State a benefit.**
Example: 'Which means to you that you will give your people cutting-edge tools that will massively increase both their confidence and their ability to persuade.'
Here you are stating a benefit you know they would most likely want. But you are about to take it further, much further.

Step 4:   **AND WHAT THAT REALLY MEANS TO YOU IS … – State a benefit.**
Example: 'And what that really means to you is a major increase in turnover and market share, which will make both your people and your management very, very happy.'
Here you are stating an even deeper, stronger, or more personal benefit.

Step 5:   **AND THE REASON WHY I SAY THAT IS … – State evidence.**
Example: 'I've already achieved this for several companies like yours in South Africa. Companies such as … have made use of my services, with magnificent results. Here are specific case studies and results: …'
Here you need to provide evidence for your claims. This evidence can be testimonials, such as examples and facts about the market.

Step 6:   **Get permission to PROBE.**
Example: 'My purpose right now is to get your answers to some questions. May I ask them?'

By the time you have finished building the six units of interest, you are ready to enlist the customer, to begin probing for problems and magnifying the hurt.

Salesplay: Creating interest

Prepare at least three six-step formulas for creating units of interest and practise them on new prospects.

Congratulations!!

I want to congratulate you for making it this far. You have demonstrated your commitment to being outstanding. You have hung in there when everybody else has let go. Take a minute to celebrate yourself, your determination, your stamina and your will to succeed.

By now, you've mastered the art of preparing and doing your homework, you know how to turn yourself on, you know how to make contact with prospects and get their attention, you're a champion at connecting and becoming their best friend and you now can create massive interest. It's time to enlist the prospect.

The ten steps to sales mastery

Phase Two
The enlist phase

Step 6:

Qualify your prospects: probe for problems and magnify the hurt

If you are running blind, you will run into a wall of rejection!

Selling is one of the most enjoyable and rewarding parts of anyone's job; it is also a fun-filled profession on one condition: You must see yourself as a finder and filler of people's real needs and desires. I believe that if you see yourself as a giver in your relationships with people and customers and not as a taker, you will experience joy, self-esteem and lots of money. One of the reasons why I love presenting, selling and motivating people is that my focus is not on me; my focus is on the value that I want to give to the people who have come to hear me. My energy is focused outwards, not inwards.

The reason why many people experience selling as a pressure activity is because they are trying to persuade others to do something without passionately wanting to help them and not themselves. Without knowing who the other person really is, how they make decisions and what their real needs and desires are. Do you? Are you applying a one-size-fits-all approach to selling or persuading? Or do you have an emotional blueprint for understanding your prospect?

Without an emotional blueprint of the person you're selling to, you're running blind. And if you're running blind, you're liable to run into a wall of rejection. When I review my failures in selling and motivating, I can see clearly that they happened because I didn't understand the emotional blueprint of my prospect or delegates.

The challenge is to qualify the prospect in the initial sales call by asking several questions that will determine his or her main needs, interests and beliefs. You are the kind of person who has done their homework and you're turned on, so you're ready to ask the right questions. You're confident. You're eager. You're enthusiastic. You're having fun. You've connected with the prospect. You're ready to rock and roll! Am I right? Of course.

The key is to understand how the prospect thinks and feels. What are their beliefs, how do they look at the world, what do they really desire most and what are their needs? As soon as you know this information, you have tremendous power and very little fear of being rejected. You will know how to anticipate the way they think and take appropriate, proactive action.

Achtung! Warning! Waarskuwing: Never, ever attempt to challenge someone else's beliefs. Often, a prospect's beliefs about what you can sell them can be as deep-set as their own religious convictions. Even if you have a lifetime at your disposal, you may not be able to change someone's beliefs, so don't attempt to change them in an hour. Instead, as we have already explored, make your ideas consistent with the prospect's beliefs. Remember to align and redirect.

The purpose of this session is to help you to develop a simple, systematic program for finding out who you are dealing with, what they really want and need, and how they make decisions or justify taking action. With this information, selling becomes enjoyably easy.

NWWAM, WHY and HOW

As you qualify the prospect, probe for problems and magnify the hurt, all you have to know is NWWAM, WHY and HOW. Memorize it. It's easy: NWWAM, WHY and HOW. Say it aloud; it sounds great: NWWAM!! Keep this little acronym with you as you qualify the prospect in your initial meetings before you even go for the close.

NWWAM stands for the five answers you want to know as quickly as possible when you are in the stage of qualifying the prospect. Let's look at each one in turn (and by the way, as I take you through NWWAM, do a little self-exploration: Answer these questions about yourself as well):

1 **Needs:** What does the prospect really need? Remember that people buy on emotion but justify on needs – remember LRBN (Logical Reasons to Buy Now). What is the prospect's LRBN? If you can meet their LRBN, you give them permission to justify what they really want. (What are *your* needs?)

2 **Wants:** What does the prospect really want? What is the emotional desire that needs to be met? What are their ERBN (Emotional Reasons to Buy Now)? Are they buying a car because it's transport or because it's a badge? Are they buying your service because they want a reliable service provider or are they really looking for a friend? Are they buying you because your proposal meets their specs or are they buying you because you are the one most likely to make them look good to their management? Are they buying you because of your ability to deliver or are they buying you because your company is seen to be a winner? (What are *your* wants?)

3 **Wounds:** What does the prospect have pain about? What do they feel like they really want but aren't getting out of life? Remember that people are more motivated to avoid pain than to gain pleasure. If you can open a wound and show them how to heal it through you and your product, you'll create a very motivated buyer. What are they really scared about? What are they angry about? What are they frustrated about? What are

they confused about? What do they think other people or companies have that they don't have? What are their DRAB (Dominant Reasons to Avoid Buying)? (What are *your* wounds?)

4　**Authority:** Do they have the authority to make the decision? This is vital information that you need to find out upfront, rather than after you have made the presentation. Even if they don't have the authority, you may still decide to proceed with the presentation if you believe that they can strongly influence the ultimate purchase decision. Once you discover this information, your presentation will not be aimed at closing the prospect, but merely motivating them to take the buying process to the next level. You have to know the length and breadth of the buying cycle: how long it takes, how many people are involved and the nature of the decision-making process. (Do *you* have the authority or the will to make decisions there and then? Are you prepared or empowered to do whatever it takes to make the sale? Or do you have to check with 'head office'?)

5　**Money:** Do they have the money? If there is absolutely no way for them to obtain the money, you may be wasting your time. However, if you believe that they may have the money at a later point in time, then you may wish to continue. However, it will save you a lot of heartache and frustration if you find out what their financial situation is *before* you make your sales pitch. (How much are *you* prepared to invest in making the sale?)

In addition to NWWAM, you also want answers to WHY and HOW:

6　**Why:** Why do they want these things and why do they have these wounds? It's not enough just to know that they want a particular car or house or investment. You have to know WHY they want it. This means understanding their beliefs and values, which we'll explore later in this session. (Why do *you* do what you do?)

7　**How:** How do they go about making their decisions? How do they know when they are getting what they want? What kind of evidence do they need? For example, how do they know a car is fast: Is it because it goes from zero to 60 in five seconds; is it because their friends say it's fast or is it because of the feeling they get when they're in the car? (How do *you* make decisions?)

You can create an emotional blueprint of people and magnify their hurt by asking the seven key emotional blueprint questions that are described above:

1 What does the prospect really need? What are their LRBN?
2 What does the prospect really want? What are their ERBN?
3 What are their wounds and fears? What are their DRAB?
4 Do they have the authority to make the decision or are they merely an influencer?
5 Do they have the money or can they get the money?
6 Why do they want what they want?
7 How do they make their buying decision?

If you think about your key prospects and customers, do you have the answers to the seven emotional blueprint questions? If you do, treat this session as a refresher course. You are already a Champion Salesperson! If not, start answering them now.

WHY: values — the ultimate motivators

Throughout this book, I have consistently spoken about the vital importance of values. In the first session, I spoke about the necessity of understanding your own values. Then, in the session on rapport and questions, I spoke about the necessity of understanding your prospect's values. Values are what ultimately motivate people. Values determine the way we feel about anything. And the way we feel about anything, in turn, determines the decisions we make. If you want to persuade someone to make a particular decision, you first have to understand why it is they do what they do. If you can convince somebody WHY they should do something, the HOW is easy.

As I said before, pain and pleasure are the Siamese twins of human motivation. Think about this right now: What gives you pleasure and what gives you pain? What do you want more than anything else in the world? What really winds your clock? What really turns you on? On the other hand, what do you hate the most in the world? What will you do anything to avoid?

Would you agree that having the answers to the preceding questions gives you an insight into why you do what you do? And would you agree that if you knew what turned your customer on and off, it would also give you the Abracadabra to their heart? Definitely! So let's take a final advanced class in understanding and managing people's values.

'Towards' values versus 'away' values

All of us have values that we associate with pleasure and values that we associate with pain. A 'towards' value is a value that will take us where we want to go. An 'away' value is a value that takes us where we don't want to go; it is an emotional state that we want to avoid at any cost. An important towards value of mine is courage: If I have courage, I will achieve what I want to achieve. An away value of mine is depression: If I get depressed, it means maximum pain for me, because that means I will go back to the hell that I was in for three years. Right now, think about five towards values and five away values you have. At this stage of the book, you should be able to do this with ease.

The 'open sesame' of selling

The first 'open sesame' or guarantee of success in selling that I told you about is simply increasing the number of times you get in front of a prospect. The second 'open sesame' is as follows: *You want to show the prospect how investing in your product or service will help them to achieve their towards values. You also want to show the prospect how investing in your product will help them to avoid their away values.*

The key element in probing for people's problems and magnifying the hurt, therefore, is finding out what that hurt is. Here's an elegant and trust-building way in which to do that (begin using this approach as soon as possible – it's very powerful): 'I'm not like other salespeople. I really want to meet your needs and deliver what you want. In order to do that, I'd like to ask you a couple of questions about what is most important to you. If I can understand what is most important to you in life and in this area of business, then I know I can really help you to meet your needs. Is it okay if we take a couple of minutes to do this?'

This approach will surprise and delight the customer because what you are demonstrating is that you are interested in them as a person first and foremost. Then you follow up with these questions:

☛ What's most important to you in life? Why?
☛ What else is important to you? Why?
☛ What's most important to you when it comes to ...? Why?
☛ What else is important to you? Why?
☛ What do you want most in life? Why?
☛ What do you want most in your job? Why?
☛ What do you want most when it comes to dealing with suppliers? Why?
☛ What are the things you want to avoid? Why?

You can also discover what people's towards values are by looking around their office:

☛ What's on their walls?
☛ What's on their desk?
☛ What other clues are there to your prospect's values?

I would like to share with you two success stories of mine that highlight the merit of playing to the prospect's towards values:

I recently made a presentation to a prospect whose wall was full of photos of him playing golf with colleagues. He was a golf fanatic. All he wanted to do was get out there on the greens. The first thing he said to me when I walked into his office was, 'I'm really busy right now. I don't have much time!' My response was, 'That's exactly why I want to talk to you – because I know you're busy and I'm sure you'd rather be playing golf than listening to me. Would you want to hear about something that could help you do that? Would that be pretty important to hear about?' Needless to say, he listened and I eventually made the sale.

The second success story is about a prospect I wanted to persuade to hire me for a series of motivational sessions across the country. The only problem was that he was speaking to four other candidates for the assignment. I knew I needed the edge.

And then I found it. I saw an Air Zimbabwe plane ticket on his desk, so I asked him why he was going to Zimbabwe. He told me he was going bungee jumping off a bridge near the Victoria Falls. The moment I heard this, I knew one of his values must be adventure, getting an adrenaline rush and excitement. I adjusted my sales pitch immediately. I said to him that if he hired me, 'It will take a leap of faith. We'll take your people to the edge. We'll jump boldly into the unknown and go where we've never gone before!' Needless to say, I connected with his towards values in a big way and I got the business!

HOW: discover your client's buying strategies – their patterns of focus

Every day we are bombarded with stimuli. Our world is changing at an accelerating pace. Images, sounds, movements and smells are all vying for our attention continuously. At any moment in time, there are a number of things we could focus on. Every second, there are hundreds of things that demand our attention.

In order to stay sane, our conscious mind (with its limited ability to focus) has developed strategies for limiting the number of things we focus on and make decisions about. It has done this by creating *patterns of focus*. For example, when you walk into a room, you don't usually evaluate whether you will remain vertical and whether the floor will hold you up (unless you're on a boat or you're inebriated). You take that for granted and you focus on other things. The value of this is that it saves us time and energy so that we *can* focus on other things.

People also develop buying patterns to conserve time and energy. People develop patterns of what to focus on when they make a decision. Some people focus on cost, some focus on convenience, some focus on benefits, some focus on what they might lose out on. Their pattern of focus will determine what you need to do in order to persuade them most convincingly.

I'll now share with you a fascinating, powerful tool: Discover your prospect's buying pattern so that you can align with it and sell like you've never sold before. The key to using this tool is asking the right questions and listening intensely. Use the ten key patterns of focus to focus yourself on your client (as we move through the ten key patterns of focus, also ask yourself what your patterns of focus are):

The ten key patterns of focus

1   **Is your prospect a mover towards or a mover away?** Some of us make decisions primarily to avoid pain while some of us make decisions to gain pleasure. Listen to your customer. Do they focus on the pain of not doing something or the pleasure to be derived from doing it? In my case, I'm a mover towards. I do things because of what I can achieve. I will not be motivated by the possibility of loss. In fact, if someone says to me, 'If you don't do this, you'll miss out!' I get irritated. (What are *you*?)

2   **Does your prospect use an internal or an external frame of reference?** Some people go inside themselves to decide if something is right. It's very simple for you to find out. Ask the questions 'How do you know when you've done a great job?' and 'How will you know this is right for you?' In my case, I use an internal frame primarily. (What do *you* use?)

3   **Is your prospect a necessity or a possibility kind of person?** Some people need to be shown that it's absolutely necessary before they buy. Others are driven simply by the possibility of making something happen. I'm a possibility person. You can find out simply by asking the

question 'If I told you this was possible, would you be interested?' (What kind of person are *you*?)

4   **Is your prospect a matcher or a mismatcher?** Matchers are people who look for sameness; they look for how things are alike. Mismatchers look for how things are different. You can discover your prospect's pattern of focus by listening to whether they look for differences or similarities between things. How many times do they contradict you? I'm a matcher. (What are *you*?)

5   **Is your prospect a self-sorter or an other-sorter?** A self-sorter is someone who focuses primarily on themselves. Their main concern is the impact that things will have on themselves. An other-sorter is someone who focuses primarily on others. A self-sorter uses the words 'I', 'me', 'my', 'mine'. An other-sorter uses the words 'we', 'us', 'ours'. I've become an other-sorter. (What are *you*?)

6   **Is your prospect a process or a completion person?** A process person is someone who enjoys the process. A completion person is someone who just wants to finish the job. The question to ask here is: 'What do you enjoy most in life: getting things done, or do you enjoy getting involved in the process?' A process person has more patience than a completion person. As a rule, women tend to be more process people and men tend to be more completion people. However, I'm becoming a process person. (What are *you*?)

7   **Is your prospect a visual, auditory or kinesthetic person?** Does your prospect have to see, hear or feel something to believe it? Besides listening to the way they talk, you can ask them: 'How do you know if something is true? Do you have to see it for yourself? Do you have to hear it? Do you have to do it?' I'm primarily a visual person but I have strong auditory preferences. (What are *you*)?

8   **Is your prospect a generalist or a specifist?** The generalist looks at the big picture. The specifist looks at the details. Besides listening intently, here is a simple question to ask your prospects: 'Do you want the big picture or do you want the details?' I'm a generalist. (What are *you*?)

9   **Is your prospect a past or a future kind of person?** A past kind of person needs assurances about how long something has been around. A fu-

ture kind of person needs to know what you can create tomorrow. I'm a future kind of person. (What are *you*?)

10 **Is your prospect driven by cost or by convenience?** What's more important to your prospect: cost or convenience? Ask: 'Would it be worth a slight extra charge for the convenience of ...?' I'm a convenience kind of person. (What are *you*?)

If you understand your customer's pattern of focus, how they make their buying decisions, you can align with them. You can think and reason the way they do. They'll relate to you. They'll respond to you. They'll like you. They'll buy from you. Aren't you excited right now about all the ways you now have to take your ability to persuade to the next level? Aren't you excited about becoming a Champion Salesperson? Hey, don't wait! Go persuade someone about something now!

Salesplay: NWWAM, WHY and HOW
- ☛ Do an emotional blueprint of your ten key customers and prospects.
- ☛ Identify the major towards values and away values of your ten key customers and prospects. Adapt your sales pitch accordingly.
- ☛ Identify the key patterns of focus of your ten key customers and prospects. Adapt your approach accordingly.

I am extremely interested in knowing the outcome of these three salesplays for you. Let me know by writing to me: Mike Lipkin, PO Box 41882, Craighall, 2024, Johannesburg, South Africa, or you can e-mail me at lipkin@iafrica.com.

The ten steps to sales mastery

Phase Two
The enlist phase

Step 7:

Create conviction and test close

Give your prospects the certainty of their convictions

There are five emotional states that you need to take the prospect through to get them to be your customer. You have to:
☛ get their attention.
☛ get them to like you.
☛ get them interested.
☛ get them to feel a want or a need.
☛ get them to feel conviction that your product can fulfil their need or heal their 'hurt'.

The whole purpose of this step is to convince the customer that they are justified in buying. We have to create enough reasons for the prospect to feel certainty that you and your service will satisfy or even exceed their needs.

The purpose of creating conviction is to present the facts or features of your product or service in such a way that the prospect not only sees the benefits, but feels the state that they really desire.

Remember that a Champion Salesperson is a state inducer: The Champion Salesperson puts the prospect in the state they want to be in as a result of buying their product. Remember: *People don't buy facts, they don't buy features, they don't even buy benefits – they buy their most desired states!*

As a result of completing this session, you will:
☛ be able to create and apply 'units of conviction' to outweigh any fears the prospect might have to buy from you.
☛ be able to use 'test closes' to measure and know exactly where you are in the selling process. One of the biggest mistakes any salesperson can ever make is to ask for the sale before the customer is ready. In selling, as in life, timing is everything.

What have we done so far?
☛ We are prepared!
☛ We are turned on!
☛ We've made contact!
☛ We are connected!
☛ We have their interest!
☛ We have qualified them!

Now we go for the conviction!

You cannot give what you do not have:
if you are not convinced, how can you convince the prospect?

We need to convince the customer that they are justified in buying. We can do this first and foremost through congruency (the third master tool of persuasion). Your own level of belief or certainty will convince people most. Congruency happens when what you're saying on the outside is what you are feeling on the inside.

Secondly, you must absolutely believe in your brain, heart and gut that you are a *giver* not a *taker*. You must believe that what you have to offer is *ten* times more valuable than what you are asking back. When I stand up and motivate people across South Africa, I keep saying to myself, 'If I can change just one person's life in this room; if I can empower someone to get strong by taking on their fear; if I can help someone to love and not fear; if I can get one person to turn their panic into excitement, I will have delivered more value than I could ever be paid for.'

People buy for emotional reasons. ***All selling is a transfer of emotions.*** For someone to be convinced by you, you have to be convinced by yourself. Your level of conviction is the single most powerful thing you can transfer to the person that you are selling to. You have to make them feel certain, absolutely certain, that if they invest in your service, they are going to get what they want most and that it will be worth it.

Building units of conviction

We have to take the units of interest further to creating units of conviction. The whole process is as follows, starting with the units of interest:

Step 1:   State a BIG FAT CLAIM.
           Example: 'I can help you to increase your sales and productivity from 30 per cent to 300 per cent!'
           It has to be a big fat claim that the prospect really believes is valuable. The response of the customer must be 'Wow!' And it must be a claim you can back up.

Step 2:   BECAUSE – State a feature.
           Example: 'Because what I teach in my programmes are groundbreaking sales and persuasion techniques modelled on the world's master persuaders and salespeople. South Africans have never been exposed to these techniques before.'

Here I back up the big fat claim with a fact. The word I use in this transition is 'because'.

Step 3:   WHICH MEANS TO YOU – State a benefit.
Example: 'Which means to you that you will give your people cutting-edge tools that will massively increase both their confidence and their ability to persuade.'

Here you are stating a benefit you know they would most likely want. But you are about to take it further, much further.

Step 4:   AND WHAT THAT REALLY MEANS TO YOU IS ... – State a benefit.
Example: 'And what that really means to you is a major increase in turnover and market share, which will make both your people and your management very, very happy.'

Here you are stating an even deeper, stronger, or more personal benefit.

Step 5:   AND THE REASON WHY I SAY THAT IS ... – State evidence.
Example: 'I've already achieved this for several companies like yours in South Africa. Companies such as ... have made use of my services, with magnificent results. Here are specific case studies and results: ...'

Here you need to provide evidence for your claims. This evidence can be testimonials, examples, facts about the market, and so on.

Step 6:   Get permission to PROBE.
Example: 'My purpose right now is to get your answers to some questions. May I ask them?'

By the time you have finished building the six units of interest, you are ready to enlist the customer, to begin probing for problems and magnifying the hurt.

Now we add steps 7, 8 and 9 to 'test close':

Test close 1

Step 7: 'In your opinion, do you feel ...?'
Feedback no. 1.

Test close 2

Step 8: 'In your opinion, do you feel ...?'
        Feedback no. 2.

Test close 3

Step 9: 'In your opinion, do you feel ...?'
        Feedback no. 3.

Step 10: Close: assume the sale!

Steps 7, 8 and 9 build units of conviction that give the prospect compelling evidence to buy. They are test closes. And the best evidence is when the customer gives it to you because you have asked them a question.

The difference between a test close and a close

A close question is a question that can only be answered if the prospect has decided to buy. It is a *decision-making question*. A test close question is an *opinion-asking question*.

Test closing is a vital skill for Champion Salespeople to master. *How to close* is easy. *When to close* is the real question. Never close until the prospect is ready to buy.

When you ask a test close question, you are getting the prospect to make a commitment to you because they are giving you evidence why they should buy. For example, in step 7 of building units of conviction, I might say, 'In your opinion, if I could prove that I could improve your salespeople's productivity by 40 per cent or more, would that be a good reason to send your entire sales force to my programme?' In this instance, if the prospect says yes, he's begun to commit to me. If he says no, I simply probe some more and ask, 'Why are you saying that?'

From my experience and from the Champion Salespeople I have observed, however, the moment you say 'in your opinion', you take away the pressure to decide and you allow your prospect to operate without any pressure.

A normal close would be: 'Do you want it in blue or green?' or 'Do you want to start on Thursday or Friday?' or 'Do you want to send 20 or 30 people?' Ways to turn these into test closes would be to say: 'In your opinion, do you like green or blue better?' or 'If you were going to go ahead, would it be on Monday or Thursday?' or 'Just suppose you were going to go with this, would you send 20 or 30 people?'

People will respond to these questions. What a test close does is let you find out where the buyer is in terms of motivation to buy. You will notice whether they respond in a cold or hot way. Test closes help you get the 'noes' out early and minimize the risk of rejection. You can use the key words 'just suppose' whenever someone starts to give you a rejection, for example: 'Well, just suppose we managed to work that out, could we go ahead and make this deal?' Remember the ABC of selling: **Always Be** Test Closing!

The four types of test closes

The opening test close

This is where you start the presentation by finding out where the buyer is: this test close will not only tell you what their level of enthusiasm is, but also the motivation behind it. These are examples of opening test close questions:

☞ How long have you been considering owning?
☞ Are you seriously considering buying?
☞ Why are you seriously thinking of buying?

The trade-off test close

These are used as a way to see in advance if you can get the prospect to let go of their objection or fear by focusing on the state or benefit they can achieve by moving ahead. You are taking them past their DRAB to see their ERBN and LRBN. These are examples of trade-off test close questions:

☞ Would it be worth R8 000 in order to earn R75 000 in the next year?
☞ In order for you to achieve your goals, would it be worth a one-time investment of R8 000?
☞ Would it be worth spending one day with me so you can increase your income for the rest of your life?

The progressive test close

This is a way to move the prospect ahead when you seem to be at a near standstill in the attempted sale. It should be used with caution because you do not want to be perceived as pressurizing the prospect. These are examples of progressive test close questions:

☛ If you were to go ahead with this, when would you want the service to begin?

☛ If we were to overcome that problem, you would probably want to go ahead with this investment, wouldn't you?

☛ In your opinion, does this sound like something you would like to go ahead with?

The ongoing test close

This is a test close that you use throughout the session so that you can continually track your prospect's level of motivation and understanding of your presentation. These are examples of ongoing test close questions:

☛ How does that sound to you?

☛ Do you see what I mean?

☛ Does that make sense?

☛ What do you think of what I've said so far?

If you get a 'No!' answer to your test closes, that's great! Firstly, because the law of reciprocation has come into play. The more 'noes' you get, the more the prospect will owe you a 'Yes!' And secondly, a 'no' allows you to probe for more information. For example, if you get a 'no', ask, 'Do you mind if I ask why you say ...' or 'I'm curious, why would you say no to that?' or 'I respect that, but I am very interested: Why do you say no?'

Key buying signs

There are certain key non-verbal buying signs you need to be aware of while you are building units of conviction. These are:

☛ The prospect suddenly relaxes during the presentation.

☛ They have their hands open towards you.

☛ They have a sparkle in their eye.

☛ They keep putting their hand near their chin.

☛ They keep touching your literature or the product itself.

☛ They become extremely friendly.

☛ They start talking as if they are already using the service.

☛ They smile and nod their heads up and down.

☛ They pull their pen out as if to sign.

When you test close and the prospect is noticeably low in energy or uninterested, immediately start adding more conviction! Test closes are invaluable even if the client seems uninterested or not ready to buy. You always need to know where the client is during the presentation, so that you can add more ERBNs and LRBNs when necessary.

When I deliver my half-day or full-day sessions, I continually track my audience's involvement. If it's low, I'll dial up my conviction or I'll get them energized through physical movement or a joke. It's vital that you know when your customers or prospects are with you and when you've lost them, so that you can take appropriate action. Does that make sense? Are you with me so far? Are you convinced?

Salesplay: Creating conviction and test close

☛ Create at least three units of conviction right now. You can use the units of interest you created in step 5 as a starting point.

☛ Create three opening test closes, trade-off test closes, progressive test closes and ongoing test closes. Start practising as soon as possible.

The ten steps to sales mastery

Phase Three
The compel phase

Step 8:
Make it real and assume the sale

We've come a long way together; we've got just a short way to go

I am delighted that you are still with me. I am proud of you. And I am proud of me for keeping your attention, interest and conviction. We've come a long way together. We've still got just a little way to go.

We got ourselves prepared. We did our homework. We turned ourselves on. We made contact and got the prospect's attention. We connected with them personally. We built rapport. We created interest. We qualified them by probing for their problems and magnifying their hurt. We found out who they really are. We know their needs, wants, wounds, authority and money situation. We know why they do what they do and we know how they make their buying decisions. We've also built massive amounts of conviction to overcome their fears and reluctance to purchase. As a result, we now have someone who is engaged and enlisted. The final stage is to compel them to buy. It's time to get them to go all the way!

We are three steps away from achieving our goal. We will:

☛ make it real for them, bring it alive and assume the sale. If there are any difficulties when that happens, we need to convert any objections into commitments. This is a very simple process.

☛ make it easy to buy.

☛ create a future so that this isn't the end of the relationship, but the beginning of a very long, mutually profitable and enjoyable one.

Let's move on to making it real and assuming the sale.

Unleash the power of your prospect's imagination

'**imagination:** the action of forming mental images of what is not actually present to the senses; the power of reproducing images stored in the memory under the suggestion of associated images; the power of recombining former experiences in the creation of new images directed at a specific goal or aiding in the solution of problems; the ability to meet and resolve difficulties; resourcefulness'

– WEBSTER'S DICTIONARY

We have built the prospect's conviction that they should make the purchase. The challenge is to take that conviction and bring it to life. In order to get people to act, we have to unleash their imagination. Remember: *Imagination is more powerful than actual facts in driving human emotion.*

Our imagination is what we are capable of doing with the facts. If you can fire up your prospect's imagination, you can control their buying behaviour.

The purpose of this session is to help you to compel your prospect to buy your product or service by persuading them that *buying means heaven* and that *not buying means hell*.

Make it vividly real!

Make the experience of using your service or owning your product so real the prospect can see, feel, smell, hear and taste what your service or product is going to give them. Making the experience real – in advance of the prospect buying – creates a compelling reason to purchase and momentum to buy. If the client cannot mentally and emotionally visualize and experience the benefits of your offering, they probably won't buy. To quote the Webster's Dictionary, you have to help the prospect to form 'mental images of what is not actually present to the senses'. If you have worked through the seven previous steps, you now have prospects with conviction, who are logically and emotionally convinced they should buy the product. All that they now need is momentum; they need a final push. They have to feel that if they buy, it's going to be heaven, and if they don't, it's going to be hell.

If a prospect can't experience the emotions that are brought on by enjoying the benefits of your service or product; if that experience is not real in their mind, they're probably not going to go over the edge and buy.

Five ways to take control of your prospect's imagination

Sell with all five senses. Champion Salespeople don't just tell their prospect about the product: They put them in a state. Remember to play to your prospect's dominant sense. Think of the last time a salesperson really got you hot for their product. What did they do? Think of the Champion Salespeople you know. What do they do? The most successful Master Persuaders make magic with their customers. They induce powerful feelings. They take control of their prospect's head and heart. Observe great persuaders and model yourself on their success – remember that success leaves clues.

Champion Salespeople use the following five ways to take control of their prospect's imagination (by the way, ask yourself how effectively I've used the following five points throughout the book):

1 **They are great storytellers.** They tell their prospects about how other people have benefited from their services in a way that is vivid, emo-

tional and motivational to the prospect. By telling their story, they get their prospects to rehearse using or owning their product *in advance*.

2 **They use humour.** Master Persuaders have learned to put the prospect at ease and to make them smile. They get their prospects to associate their upbeat mood with them being there and with what they're selling.

3 **They are creative.** Champion Salespeople are constantly looking for new ways to make their sales pitches more compelling. They experiment with novel ideas all the time. They learn as they go.

4 **They skilfully direct their sales pitches to focus on the prospect's hurt and wounds.** Champion Salespeople are always directing their stories to disturb their prospect's wounds. However, they do it in an elegant and unobtrusive manner. They then 'heal' the hurt with their stories.

5 **They have a highly infectious energy level.** Champion Salespeople 'glow' with energy. Their mere presence animates the prospect. When they are in front of their customers, they have no doubts and no negativity. They never bad-mouth anything or anyone.

The P-T-P plan: the guaranteed way to get your prospect to experience the pleasure and the results of using your service in advance

If I could show you a guaranteed way to compel your prospect to buy by making the benefits and state he will experience real for him, wouldn't you find this valuable? If you could always depend on a formula for effective selling when you needed it most, wouldn't you want to know what it is? Well, here's your reward for making the journey with me so far: The P-T-P plan.

The P-T-P plan has three simple steps: point, tell, paint

1 Point

When you point, you highlight what the prospect wants. You point out the key benefit they're looking for and get them in the state they want to be in.

Here's what I would say to point when I am compelling the customer to buy: 'I know that you're looking for a way to motivate your people so that they can unleash their talent and energy on their customers. And I know that if they can do that, you'll feel fulfilled because you'll see all your people being successful and having fun. That's something you want, isn't it?'

Think about how you could remind your prospect or customer of their want in such a way that it makes them feel the way they want to feel.

2 Tell

You have to tell your customer with passion and precision that your service or product will deliver the benefits and state they are looking for. It is important when you tell them that you are totally congruent. Everything about you must radiate confidence, assurance and decisiveness. Practise saying this to yourself in the mirror. Do it again and again until you manage to convince you. These are the words that I use to tell my prospects about my service – short, strong and simple: 'Well, that's exactly what my programme will do for you and your people.'

3 Paint

You further have to paint a picture of the future as a result of using your product or service. The key here is to take the prospect into the kind of result and state they will enjoy as a result of making the decision to buy (from you). When painting the picture, you have to get creative and capture the prospect's imagination by unleashing your own imagination.

This is how I would paint a picture for my prospects: 'After your people have attended my programme, their motivation and ability to persuade others will increase by 200 per cent in some cases. You'll be surrounded by people who are juiced and pumped. In fact, they'll be so pumped you'll have difficulty holding some of them back. Wouldn't that be a great change? And wouldn't it be brilliant to come to work in the morning and actually have your people get you motivated; not to mention the glowing reports you'll begin to get from your customers? Imagine what will happen to the business. I wouldn't be surprised if you record sales increase up to 50 per cent. And by the way, don't you think your board of directors will be pleased with you because of these outstanding results? The question I have for you is: Isn't this what you really want? Isn't joy and achievement what it's all about? Can you really afford not to do it? Don't you owe it to your people? Don't you owe it to yourself?' Then assume the sale!

Salesplay: Make it real

Prepare a P-T-P plan for your top ten key prospects and/or customers. Get creative. Get better and better by practising and practising.

The ten steps to sales mastery

Phase Three
The compel phase

Step 9:

Convert objections into commitments

The most feared word in selling: No! *Nyet! Non! Nee!*

Most salespeople are more scared of the tiny word 'no' than they are of any other word. The fear of objections or rejection when the customer says: 'No, I don't want you or your products,' is almost as great as the fear of death itself. I'm not overexaggerating. The fear of failure is really the fear of rejection. And have you ever noticed how we will do anything to avoid that which we fear the most?

No book on selling and persuasion would be complete without a session on handling objections. You would expect that. However, I'm going to go beyond your expectations, way beyond them.

How would you feel if you could walk into any selling or prospecting situation and actually look forward to objections? How confident would you be if you had a powerful system for converting any objection into a commitment? Do you think it would make a difference in the amount of calls you made or prospects you canvassed? Would it take a weight off your mind? Would you like to know the ultimate Abracadabra of selling? Do I hear you shouting: 'Yes! Yes! Yes!'?

As a result of completing this session, you will have mastered a nine-step formula for handling any objection and converting it into a commitment. If you apply what I share with you here, you'll become a CHOC: a Champion Objection Converter!

Are you ready? Let's do the second last step to sales mastery!

What is an objection?

From now on, see objections as the most valuable thing the prospect can do for you, for these reasons:

☛ It gives you an opportunity to know what's really going on in the customer's mind.

☛ It is an opportunity to understand someone else's beliefs and doubts. When they object, they are really sharing their fears with you at that particular moment.

☛ Objections are really questions in disguise. They are requests for more information and assurances.

☛ Objections give you the opportunity to test close as well as to really close.

☛ Objections give you a chance to align with the customer. Never, ever fight an objection: Align with it. Use it as an opportunity to build empathy with the customer.

Nine steps to handle any objection

Step 1: Ignore it.

Why ignore it? Simply because the prospect may not mean it. We often say 'no' because we're on automatic pilot. It's easier to say 'no' than to say 'yes'. If a customer says to me, 'You're too expensive,' my first response is just to look at them, maybe even smile a little and remain silent. Don't feel the need to immediately defend your fee or price. Maybe the objection isn't real. Just let it fly by. Go with the flow.

Step 2: Hear the person out.

The prospect may run out of steam if you give them time to have their say. Many salespeople are so eager to defend their product that they don't give the prospect a chance to just let their feelings come out.

Have you ever noticed that when some people are really upset, if you just shut up and listen to them – really sincerely listen to them – they will eventually run out of steam and answer their own objection?

When people tell me I'm too expensive, and they're uptight because they really want me but they had a preconception about what my fee would be, I just listen to them. Often they will talk themselves into accepting my fees.

Step 3: Feed it back nicely.

Feed the objection back with a question in a tone of empathy and friendliness. I will just say, 'Too expensive?' The prospect now has to explain to you why it's too expensive.

Often they just give up or even convince themselves that you're actually not too expensive.

Step 4: Align with the prospect and question the objection.

Show that you have empathy with the client, while politely getting permission to challenge the objection, for example: 'You and I both know that you have reasons for saying that – would it be okay if I asked you what they are?'

Notice that I didn't say that the prospect had good reasons: just reasons. You now have an idea of what the prospect's beliefs, doubts and fears are.

Step 5: **Make it a final objection.**

The way we make it a final objection is to use the 'as if' frame and test close. (Revisit the session on framing skills.) Listen strongly. When people tell you the reasons for the objections, you now have the power to close the sale because you now know what is really motivating them. Here's what I would say in the situation where the prospect has said I'm too expensive: 'If we were able to come to terms on the fee, would you definitely hire me for your conference?'

If the prospect says 'yes', I would find a creative way to reach a win-win on the fee and attempt to close the sale. If the prospect hesitates, I would ask why and go back to step 3. In most selling situations or negotiations, though, there is more than one objection. Things are not so simple. So read on.

Step 6: **Align with the prospect and sincerely acknowledge them as special people.**

Learn to dance with your prospect, not fight. If you acknowledge the fact that all people want to feel special, respected and appreciated, you will transform the way people respond to you. Remember and use these four magic phrases:

☛ I appreciate that and …
☛ I respect that and …
☛ I agree and …
☛ Other people have also said …

Never, ever say 'but' after these phrases: The moment you use the word 'but', you make the other person wrong. And you can always respect, appreciate or agree with at least one or two things the prospect has said. In my example, this is what I would say: 'I appreciate what you're saying. I respect your opinion that I might be expensive. I agree that if you haven't worked with me before and seen what I can do, you could see my fee as expensive. Other people have also felt the same way until they saw me perform.'

If you handle step 6 right, you're on the same side as the prospect. You're connected. You're enjoying each other.

Step 7: **Turn the objection into a question.**

If you change the question, you change the focus of the prospect. If you ask the right question, you can get the prospect to see your offering in a way that motivates them to purchase. You want to change their focus from the objection to a question about other positive possibilities.

Learn this phrase by heart and use it: 'That brings up the question: The question is … Isn't that the real question?' In my example where someone says I'm too expensive, I would use this step as follows: 'That brings up the question: The question is how much value are you going to get from the session? Isn't that the real question?' or 'That brings up the question: The question is will you get what you really want from your conference if you hire me? Isn't that the real question?' or 'That brings up the question: The question is can I make your conference such a success that everyone becomes supermotivated? Isn't that the real question?'

A good way to ask the question may be to open up the hurt again, to use pleasure and pain to compel the prospect to buy, for example: 'If you don't hire me and get the best, isn't it going to cost you a lot more?' or 'If the end of your conference is an anticlimax and people are demotivated, how dissatisfied will management be?'

Step 8:   Use Y TOM and ED.

Y TOM and ED is an acronym for six ways to handle any objection that might still persist at this stage of the process:

Y: Ask why.
T: Turn it around.
O: Outweigh it.
M: Minimize it.
E: Explain it.
D: Deny it.

Here's my example:

Objection: 'You cost too much!'

Ask why: 'Why are you even thinking about that right now? You just finished telling me how much your business needs me.'

Turn it around: 'That's exactly why you have to use me, because I will continue to cost too much until your business earns more money, which is exactly what I will help you do.'

Outweigh it: 'It's true, it does cost a lot, but how much will it cost if you don't do it? How much will you miss out on? What will the negative impact be on your people and the overall performance of your business?'

Minimize it: 'It is definitely an investment. However, when you consider what you spend a year on the problems associated with employee demotivation and depression, it's not that much, is it?'

Explain it: 'You're right, it is a major investment. And the reason is that you're getting one of the best motivators in the world to get your people juiced! You're buying five-star quality!'

Deny it: 'I'm no more expensive than any of the other top five speakers in the country. Here are five names for you to call and see what their quotes are. I know you'll find my fee fair.'

Think about these six ways to handle objections. Prepare them in advance. Practise them. I promise you that you will be fully armed to handle anything the prospect can throw at you. And you'll enjoy yourself more because you'll never be afraid of objections or rejections again.

Step 9: **Tie it down.**
You've handled everything. It's time to wrap it up with a simple phrase: 'That does it, doesn't it?'

Salesplay: Converting objections into commitments

Prepare a nine-point plan to convert the objections of your top ten key prospects and customers into commitments. Have fun. Practise them until you are a CHOC.

The ten steps to sales mastery

Phase Three
The compel phase

Step 10:

Assume the sale: make it easy and create a future

Congratulations!! You've made it! And so have I! We are the Champions! Hubba! Hubba! Time to bring out the champagne and celebrate! We've both made it to the end. We're part of that tiny, elite band of achievers who never, never give up. We stay the course. We get going when others are long gone. We have the stamina and the power to finish what we start.

I hope you feel really good about yourself right now. Take a moment to congratulate yourself. Give yourself credit before you set yourself yet another Big Hairy Audacious Goal.

All that remains is for us to review the last and final step towards sales mastery – assume the sale: Make it easy and create a future.

Assume the sale

You've engaged, enlisted and compelled the prospect to buy. Now you need to assume the sale by making it easy for the prospect to make that final step.

Just as I have congratulated you for making it this far, you need to congratulate the prospect on a wise decision. The sale is all but made. I'm sure if you're a professional salesperson; you already have a range of final close questions. If not, here are some that I use:

☛ 'Will I be speaking on the Monday or the Tuesday?'
☛ 'Do you want me to speak on marketing or personal motivation?'
☛ 'Can I put your company down for 20 or 25 delegates?'
☛ 'Would you like me to supply a copy of my book *Abracadabra!* or *Fire & Water* for each delegate so they can have a hard copy of my talk?'

The principle of these 'assume the sale' questions is that whatever answer the prospect gives you, they have made the decision to buy. However, remember the old adage: 'Many a slip between cup and lip.' There exists always the danger that your prospect could back out at the last moment when they are faced with the prospect of making the final, irrevocable decision to purchase.

Here are five methods to make it easy for your client to make that final decision:

1   **Celebrate them.** Make your prospect feel like something wonderful has just happened. If it's appropriate in terms of time, environment and client, literally open a bottle of bubbly or drink of the client's preference.

2   **Keep a final incentive in reserve.** You can give this to the client at the point of signing so that they stay committed to their decision. In my

case, if I'm trying to get a company to hire me, I might say to the client that I will give each person a laminated card with key points as added value, or I might offer to interview key people ahead of the session. The principle here is for you to push your prospect over the edge with a final, gentle nudge.

3 **Use contrast to make it easy.** For example, I will say: 'You're lucky you're buying now, because the price will double by the end of the year' or 'You're right to book now because this event will be a sell-out.'

4 **Make it fun. Put your prospect at ease.** If you can get someone to laugh at the end of a close, you make it easy for them.

5 **Focus on the future.** Focus on the immense future benefits the client will enjoy as a result of buying you and your product. Reassure the client on your involvement. If you offer after-sales service, reinforce it here.

Referrals: the Champion Salesperson's gold

As we've already discussed, referrals are the gold of Champion Salespeople. The best time to ask for a referral is when you have just delighted or exceeded the expectations of a customer.

Remember that one referral is worth ten cold-calls. If you ask for the referral in the right way, it can even cement your bond with the customer who has just bought from you.

I use this motivational way to ask for referrals from customers: 'The only way I'm able to build my business is through people who believe in me because I've delivered the goods for them. Those people refer me to other people they care about: friends, customers and colleagues. Have I delivered for you? Would you do me a favour in return? Can you think of a friend, client or colleague who needs a motivator or sales coach to turn themselves and their people into champions?' (You try it. See if it works for you.)

Once you get the referral, ask two more questions:
1 How do you think they could use my services?
2 What do you like most about this person?

When you meet the person you've been referred to, tell them about the compliment that the original customer paid them. You'll begin to build rapport with the person you've been referred to as well as cement your relationship with the original customer, because they will hear about it.

Keep watering the garden if you want your plants to grow!

One of the biggest mistakes many salespeople make (including me), is that we do not keep prospecting and reprospecting existing customers. This was rammed home to me recently when I met a customer who hired me two years ago. This customer said to me, 'Are you still doing your motivational sessions? We had a need for someone like you last month and we hired this woman called Jane Smith. She was good, but it's a pity we didn't think about you.' Damn right, it was a pity!

Find a way to stay in touch. One of the techniques I now use is what I call my *Top 200 File*. These are my top 200 clients. I make sure that I connect with these clients personally, telephonically or in writing every three months. Like you, I just cannot afford to let people forget about me.

Salesplay: Assume the sale and make it easy

☛ Create five ways to assume the sale with your key prospects and customers.

☛ Create five ways to nudge the client over the edge so that they don't pull out at the very last moment.

A final call to action: do it for the passion and the money will follow

In the words of Nike, 'Just Do It'. Go out there and just try out the techniques that I have shared with you in this book.

Remember that what you've been reading is the synthesis of the secrets of the world's Champion Salespeople and Master Persuaders. I just acted as the synthesizer because I wanted you to have these extraordinary techniques and strategies at your fingertips and because I love selling. Obviously I love it because it helps my company to generate revenue, but the real reason I love it is that selling really turns me on. I love persuading people and enhancing the quality of their lives. I am the luckiest person I know. I get paid to make lifelong friends because all my good customers are my great friends. And I hope you will become one too. Remember: *Apply the skills of a professional, but be driven by the passion of an amateur. Do it for the passion and the money will follow!*

Whoever you are and wherever you may be, I want to thank you once more for staying with me to the end. It means more to me than I can ever tell you. Write to me and tell me how this book has empowered you: Mike Lipkin, PO Box 41882, Craighall, 2024, Johannesburg, South Africa, or you can e-mail me at lipkin@iafrica.com.

I want to leave you with a final mantra that I say to myself every day. It has served me well; I know it will serve you:

I live in peace and security

I surrender all doubt and fear of myself,
I am never limited by past experience or present appearance.
I bless and let go of all that serves me no more,
I dare to dream anew.
I choose what rings true for me,
And I honour it with love and acceptance;
I shed every thought separating me from it.
And finally, I rest secure in the truth that sets me free:
I can be all that I can and choose to be!

Notes: